DARKEN

To Kayla,

[signature]

WHAT OTHERS ARE SAYING . . .

As a practicing veterinarian of nearly four decades, I can honestly say that I have only had the pleasure of meeting a couple of true horsemen. Those uncanny men and women who understand what makes a horse tick, and have the ability to allow the horse to become all they can be. They see potential in every horse and through patient training and enduring patience each horse blooms. These great horsemen never force a horse into a job they are not naturally suited for. The results are simply beyond amazing. Jan Sharp is one of those with this gift. Her book, *Darken: The Scaredy-Cat Champion,* captures her gift in a wonderful true story about a horse that was going to do it his way. Her experience, wisdom, and innate sixth sense for horses allowed this spirited underdog to come out on top. This is not simply a horse story. It is an essay about life. All who read it will come away refreshed and enriched.

—Charles A. Curie DVM

DARKEN: The Scaredy-Cat Champion is sure to strike a familiar chord with parents and adolescents alike who sometimes struggle to fit in and make a difference. Darken's early challenges place him in a unique and special category that children and adults with special needs can quickly identify with. This is a must read for any parent or teen. Jan Sharp's wonderful and unparalleled observations will help those of us on the outside wanting to help a child or adult with special needs.

—Linda Myers, MA, LICDC, LPC, EAGALA Advanced.

DARKEN

The Scaredy-Cat Champion

Jan Sharp

Wild Rag Press

Photography Credits

Johnny Johnston Photography—Photo 13
ForeverWorks Equine Photography—Photo 14
Jeff Kirkbride Photography—Photo 15
BarbarasVisions Photography—Photo 39, 41
Alex Fields Photography—Photo 22, 25, 26, 45
Lori Spellman Photography—Photos 23, 30, 31, 32, 42
All other photos, including the cover, taken by either Jan or Charles Sharp

Copyediting—Charles Sharp and Mindy Lightner

ISBN: 978-0615813455

CONTENTS

		Preface	vii
Chapter	1	Great Expectations	9
Chapter	2	Pintos Everywhere	15
Chapter	3	A Trick Horse In The Making	21
Chapter	4	The Bucket Disaster	33
Chapter	5	Spotty	38
Chapter	6	The Accident	41
Chapter	7	Into The Show Ring	46
Chapter	8	The Journey	49
Chapter	9	World Championship	52
Chapter	10	The Photo	57
Chapter	11	A Star Is Born	61
Chapter	12	Shall We Try Again	64
Chapter	13	The Operation	67
Chapter	14	More Than A One Trick Pony	72
Chapter	15	First Real Performance	76
Chapter	16	Hitting The Trails	80
Chapter	17	The Fish	91
Chapter	18	The Gift	97
Chapter	19	Dressage Practice	100
Chapter	20	First Dressage Show	105

Chapter 21	Putting On The Ritz	112
Chapter 22	And Away We Go	116
Chapter 23	The Quiet Horse	122
Chapter 24	Second Dressage Show	125
Chapter 25	Third Dressage Show	129
Chapter 26	The Trail Ride	134
Chapter 27	The Fun Show	139
Chapter 28	Back To The Trails	144
	Author Bio	154

PREFACE

I never met the man in person, but Roy Rogers changed my life. Watching Roy and his palomino horse, Trigger, on the silver screen, put me on the path to training my own trick horses for over forty years. In all those years, I thought I'd gotten pretty good at what I do. However, in every trainer's life, a horse comes along that will try his patience, a square peg that refuses to be put into a round hole. This is the true story of such a horse. Ride along and share the five-year journey by which a scaredy-cat colt found not only his own path in life, but how he could use his talents to help others. Climb aboard, hold on tight, and enjoy the ride.

Chapter 1

GREAT EXPECTATIONS

EXPECTING THIS to be just another quick peek inside the barn, I didn't even bother to put on socks, but slipped into an old pair of sneakers and ran out into the frosty darkness. For the past week, I'd made the short trip from house to barn every few hours around the clock. My best mare was due to foal any day. This was going to be her first foaling, and I wanted to be there to make sure her transition into motherhood went smoothly. Not only was she a very special mare, but the foal she was carrying had the potential to become a star—one of those *once in a life time* colts.

Her foal descended from royal blood and great things were expected of it. Its sire was a stunning black purebred Arabian with an impressive show record and pedigree, well known for siring champion offspring. Its mother was a black and white pinto Half Arabian/ Half Saddlebred, a combination of two different breeds; each bloodline containing multiple show champions. By the time she was two years old, I had already shown her to a Pinto World Championship. How could the blending of these bloodlines and my training skills fail to produce a winner? Surely it was written in the stars.

Not wanting to wake up the whole barn, I would flip on a single light by the mare's stall. She would look up at me with blinking eyes. Each time was the same. I'd expectantly look at her and she'd calmly look back at me, often with a bite of hay in her mouth, wondering why I was there in the middle of the night, again.

This time was different. As I walked into the barn, she wasn't looking at me, but was intent on something lying in a heap at her front feet. Her foal had just been born, still wet, with long legs that sprawled in every direction. It flopped around in the fresh straw on its elbows, trying to get its front legs untangled, trying to stand, while still barely able to lift its head. The foal, a colt, lay inches from her hooves and bumped his little domed head against her knees. She looked a bit puzzled as to just what he might be, sniffing first his head, then his tail. She stood transfixed, unable to take her soft brown eyes off him. Then she did what all mares do when they see their foals for the first time; she nickered to him in that special deep nicker reserved for just that one moment. The baby answered her back. That was all it took for the mare to accept and fall in love with him, and so did I.

It was early April, but the night air was still cold in northeastern Ohio and he was shivering. As I towel-dried his small unsteady body and admired his cute little face, he poked his nose out and tried to catch anything he could with his pink tongue. When he found my fingers, he latched on and sucked on them with determination. I'd seen dozens of foals born and it always amazed me how they were all born hard-wired to immediately look for food. He lay stretched out across my lap and sucked on my chin with toothless gums while his fuzzy foal whiskers tickled my face. Compared to the frosty night air, his mouth was hot and his jaws, looking for a meal, grabbed and pulled at my clothes like a pair of pliers.

I gathered him up in my arms and gave him a big hug. Not only was his coat soft as velvet, but I could practically feel the potential in him, just waiting to be discovered. He was smaller than average, his back a mere six inches wide. It was hard to imagine him ever being big enough to ride. I had begun making plans for him long before he was even born. In those eleven months from conception to birth, I had plenty of time to envision all the adventures he and I were going to share. He was going to be my future show horse, a champion in the making for sure.

I was overjoyed that this foal had inherited his mother's black and white spotted coat. He was mostly black, but on his left side, he had white markings; one shaped like a western boot, another like a pair of elk antlers, and a perfect little white square near his elbow that everyone said looked like a postage stamp. On his right shoulder was a large white marking, extending from his withers to below his elbow that looked exactly like a sea horse. He had four high white stockings, a small star on his forehead, and a snip of white on his nose. Just above his tail, was a marking that looked like a perfect pair of wings spread open for flight. It reminded me of an old proverb familiar to all Arabian horse owners...*When God created the horse he said to* the *magnificent creature: I have made thee as no other. All the treasures of the earth lie between thy eyes. Thou shalt carry my friends upon thy back. Thy saddle shall be the seat of prayers to me. And thou shalt fly without wings, and conquer without any sword; oh horse.*—Bedouin legend. I should have taken it as a warning. If horses can fly without wings, just how fast would they go *with* them?

He had a beautiful Arabian head and smooth body. I cupped one of his small wet ears in the palm of my hand. He was so new that his ears had not uncurled yet. What a privilege to have a front row seat to watch him unfold and discover himself. I couldn't have been happier...until he stood up.

It's not unusual for the legs of newborn foals to at first appear crooked. Because of the narrowness of their chests, many foals' front legs might toe out or appear to be knock-kneed, but as they fill out and grow, their legs normally will straighten up. It's also common that they might have weak flexor tendons which allow the toes of their hooves to tip up, especially in the rear legs. This colt had such weak tendons in his pasterns that when standing in front of him, you could see the bottoms of all four of his feet. As most of these foals grow and get stronger, their tendons strengthen and the problem usually corrects itself. I didn't worry about him; he just needed more time to grow.

He was still less than one hour old, but I already had his whole life planned out. This was the colt that was going to fulfill all of my dreams. Horsemen have been dreaming that same dream from the day man first discovered just how valuable horses were—for work, war, sport, and more recently, just for pleasure and companionship. It's the chasing of that dream that keeps man striving to breed that perfect horse.

My perfect horse has always been the Half Arabian tobiano-patterned pinto, which combines the beauty of the Arabian with the splashy white color pattern of the pinto. Pintos come in all base colors, from light to dark and with few spots or many, but my favorite has always been the black and white. Pintos come in basically two color patterns, the overo and the tobiano. Purebred Arabians do not come in the tobiano pattern, where the white coloring crosses somewhere over the horse's back or neck, so they must be outcrossed to a breed that does. Half Arabian tobiano pintos are horses which have one solid-colored purebred Arabian parent and the other parent, often a Paint, Saddlebred, or Half Arabian, who is a tobiano pinto. The resulting foal carries not only the look of the Arabian, but, hopefully, also inherits the pinto pattern from its pinto parent. This allows the foal to be registered in both the Half Arabian and Pinto registries. With this new foal, my wish for both black and spots had been granted.

The colt needed a name. His mother's official registered name was Spot N The Dark, but her barn name was Spotty. (I know, how original for a pinto horse.) She was nick-named for a small white star that stood out on her otherwise all black head. When she was a foal herself, in the pasture at night I would often see just her small white star, practically glowing, in the dark of her face. Her colt's registered name would be Darker N Bey, but his barn name became Darken, because of his mostly dark color. On days when he was being quirky, "The Black Fox" seemed to fit him better. His devilish little black ears, poking up from the wisps of his sparse little colt mane, were a forewarning of days to come.

Chapter 2

PINTOS EVERYWHERE

WHEN I was born, my parents already had a family horse named Lucky. He was a bay pinto gelding and was, most likely, part Saddlebred although we never knew for sure. He was tall, narrow and very regal. I learned to ride on, perhaps not-so-lucky, Lucky. My dad built a contraption in the pasture that was much like the metal ring pony-ride ponies are attached to at the fair. I could ride to my delight, while Lucky was attached to a stationary revolving ring. I spent many an hour riding around and around that circle pretending I was a great rider having daring adventures. While she washed dishes, my mother kept an eye on me from her vantage point at the kitchen window. Lucky was smart enough to mostly walk, and walk very slowly. If I worked hard enough, he might manage a slow trot for a few steps. He knew which side his bread was buttered on and he wisely took care of me. Lucky only had one fault; whenever anyone rode him outside of my little ring, no matter who they were or where they were, when he'd had enough, he went home, and he didn't stop until his nose touched the barn door. Lucky was one smart old horse; he constantly proved it by outsmarting all the kids in our neighborhood and many of their parents, who were sure they could cure him of this vice. No one ever did.

At age seven, I got my own pony. My parents paid fifty dollars for him. Apparently, no one had ever taken the time to handle him and he was terrified of us. I gave the pitiful thing the regal name of King. I have no idea why any parent would buy such a wild pony for a child, but my parents didn't seem the least bit concerned about it at the time. Under our care, King flourished and quickly grew into his name. Like Lucky, King was also a pinto. I trained him to be ridden and he, in turn, taught me how to ride better. Ponies are very good at teaching little girls how to ride, and I often had the lumps and bumps to prove it.

Soon I discovered that there was a horse show grounds not far from my neighborhood. One visit to a show and I knew my destiny. No longer content to watch others, I wanted to show my own pony in the worst way. My parents were not horse show parents; they were barely horse people at all. They used Lucky to cultivate their garden and my brother and sister used him to deliver newspapers. I was the only one in the family interested in horse shows. Always frugal with their money, there was to be no riding lessons, no trainer, and no fancy "made" show horse. I had to make do with what I had or do without. If I wanted to go to the show, I'd have to ride my pony there and carry everything I needed for the day. I must have looked quite a sight. I wouldn't have a horse trailer until after I was married. If I wanted to learn more about horses and showing, I'd have to learn it myself. I read every horse book in the library and practiced countless hours until King and I began winning ribbons. We had many great years and adventures together before I sadly outgrew him.

When I was fourteen, a friend bought a mare which had a six month old Half Arabian colt by her side. My friend wanted the mare, but had no need of the colt. So, she made a horse crazy teenage girl's dream come true and asked my parents if I would be interested in the colt. I didn't actually hear the exact conversation because the colt was to be a surprise for me. A few days later, she drove into our driveway with her red horse trailer. She opened the trailer's back door and out bolted a fuzzy spotted colt. He hit the end of the lariat around his neck and fell down in our front yard. Obviously, he hadn't had much handling, but I didn't care. I fell in love with him on the spot. The colt's name was Rickmar Farharin. He was Half Arabian by breed and, like both Lucky and King, a pinto by color pattern.

A neighbor stopped by to visit my parents a few days after I got Farharin. My mother said, "Tell him what you just got." and I said, "I got a colt." The neighbor said, "A coat?" and I said a little louder and a little clearer, "A COLT." That must have been an important moment to me because I can still see it clearly in my mind's eye. I remember sitting at the kitchen table wearing my pajamas because I had stayed home from school sick. I guess my stuffed-up nose made my voice sound funny so that when I said "colt", my neighbor heard "coat".

Odd the things we remember. I understand remembering the big events in our lives, but wonder why a misunderstanding of the words "colt" and "coat" should be saved in my memory banks for so long. Apparently, having my own colt to train, all by myself, was a bigger event in my life than I realized at the time.

Since Faharin was three years away from being old enough to ride, I spent that time trying to teach him tricks. On TV, I had seen the western movie star, Roy Rogers and his famous palomino trick horse Trigger; I tried to teach my horse some of Trigger's tricks. At that time, there were no books on how to train a trick horse. Videos hadn't even been invented yet, and like a magician, if any trainers did know how to teach a horse tricks, they were not about to share their secrets. At first, I had no idea what I was doing, but as I learned how to train Faharin through trial and error, I began to learn what worked and what didn't.

By this time we had other horses on my parents' farm, but they were just horses. Faharin was special because he was more responsive, quicker to learn, and a more willing partner. The more tricks I taught him, the better he became at everything. He was far from being Trigger, billed as the "Smartest Horse in the Movies" who had learned more than sixty tricks, but I began seeing positive results. I also discovered that the training helped us develop a closer bond and better communication. We became as one, moving and flowing together using an unseen body language, as he willingly responded to my cues.

Faharin became a respectable trick horse, a champion show horse, and most importantly, my best friend. He was in my first wedding, stuck with me when my first husband didn't, and helped me raise my son, Shawn. He was with me when I met my second husband and even pulled the carriage at our wedding. His purchase price was very little, but the companionship, loyalty, and lessons he taught me were priceless. Faharin spent twenty one years with me and is buried in a place of honor on my farm.

With each new horse I trained, I learned more and more of the benefits of trick training. It is a unique way to train horses where they are given positive rewards for making correct responses. When done correctly, trick training is fun for both horse and handler. Each trick starts out as a simple request for the horse to respond to something I want him to do. He must never "jump the gun" and perform a trick without first being asked to do so. When he responds correctly, he is praised and rewarded. The wrong response is simply ignored rather than being punished, as many common training methods still use today.

Each trick has several parts and each one has great benefits to the horse. In learning how to stand on a pedestal, he must first learn to step onto it, then stop and balance himself, and finally step off when told. I set the horse up for success by starting with a large low box that is easy for him to stand on. Once he masters that, I use different-sized pedestals to gradually reduce the pedestal's size and increase its height, thus increasing the difficulty of the trick. The learning of just this one simple trick goes a long ways towards teaching a horse obedience, confidence, balance, self-control, relaxation, and patience. These things are very important to all horses; no matter what their discipline. Even if your interest is only trail riding, time spent working with your horse to be more obedient and responsive to your aids is well worth the effort.

I really don't need another horse who knows how to stand on a pedestal but I do need one who is obedient to my cue to step up when asked. A horse who obeys the "step up" cue will never be a problem loading into a trailer or crossing a trail bridge.

Horses learn faster if there is something in it for them. In the beginning of their training, I give them small tidbits of food for making the correct response to my cues. As they begin to master a certain trick, I gradually reduce their rewards until they are getting a treat every other time, then every third time, and so on until it is eventually phased out entirely. Of course, even an advanced trick horse always appreciates a reward at the end of each training session. That reward might be a small food treat, a good scratching of his itchy spots, or a gentle pat on his forehead and a kind word. At this point the horse is working for you entirely because he wants to. It's this instilling of *wanting to* that makes trick training so beneficial. What rider doesn't want a horse who works for him because he wants to, not because he has to? Through consistent handling, fair treatment, repetition, patience, practice, and positive reinforcement, you can teach a horse to do amazing things.

As time went on, I learned that I could also use my horses to benefit other people. Even though we lived in a rural area, many children knew little about horses; in fact, many had never even touched a horse. Thus began my children's programs. I began to use my trick horses in a unique way to both entertain and teach kids about horses. Since several of my horses were rescues, they gave me the opportunity to teach kids how to care for and be kind to all animals, as well as how to recognize abuse and prevent neglect.

In time, my trick horses received invitations from all over the country to perform for groups and charity events. After each performance, we would always have a question and answer period. It never ceased to amaze me how children were always most interested in the horses' teeth and horse shoes. I guess it is something that they rarely get to see, especially if their only contact with horses is through their television set.

My goal, as a youth, was always to become famous in the horse world. As it turned out, a number of my horses did become very well known. While many of them had outstanding show careers, it was their tricks that made them stars. My most well-known horse to this point, TS Black Tie Affair, was a black and white Half Arabian pinto stallion I had shown and used in my trick act for over twenty years. In addition to being a trick horse, he earned many world championships, special awards, and was even honored by having a model toy horse made in his likeness. I, on the other hand, am known as Black Tie's mother. Well at least I am known for something!

Over the years, I climbed the horse show ladder from the bottom rung all the way up to the national level. I trained and exhibited my own horses to twenty-eight world and reserve world championships, always on a budget and always doing everything myself. It wasn't always easy, but it can be done if you want it badly enough.

Chapter 3

A TRICK HORSE IN THE MAKING

I HAVE trained dozens of trick horses, selling most and keeping some to show and exhibit myself. The ones I sold went to farms all over the country. At the time Darken was born, I had a whole barn full of horses that I used to show and most of them also performed in my trick horse act. I expected Darken to easily follow in his mother's hoof prints. Spotty was not only a world champion show horse, but an exceptional trick horse as well. She entertained and educated hundreds of children in her lifetime. Many a child's first horse experience was tentatively touching the end of her soft muzzle with one small, outstretched finger. Darken was going to be even better than she was. At least, that was the plan.

I gladly put in the time and effort necessary to raise all my colts to grow into well-rounded horses. With Darken, I planned to devote extra time, making sure he'd get a good head start in life. It was a formula that had always worked for me and I was confident in the finished product. My horses have all been calm, easy going, dependable show and trick horses; every one. Darken was to be the crowning achievement of my training career to date; I couldn't wait to get started.

Foals have very short attention spans, but they can learn simple behaviors very quickly and they seem to enjoy the extra attention. The usual things that all colts learn include being handled for grooming, clipping, hoof trimming, and being tied and led. In addition to these, I begin to teach them a few simple tricks. I encourage them to stand on a wooden box built especially for them, or I gather them up in my arms and sit down with them in a giant bean bag. They learn to enjoy human contact and to look forward to their little training sessions.

When Darken was a few days old, I placed a low wooden box in his stall. His mother would be able to stand close to him for support and comfort. She understood what the box was and she loved to stand on it herself. She proudly watched as I encouraged her first born to get closer to the box.

My other horses entertain themselves for hours with the props of my trick horse act. One mare, loose in the indoor arena for the first time with her newborn foal, took her foal straight up to the box and stepped up onto the box with both her front feet. It was very clear that she was showing her foal the purpose of the box. Her foal stood beside her and seemed bewildered, as it stared intently at what she was doing, trying to figure it out.

I gathered Darken up in my arms and began his first lesson. It was a simple trick where he just needed to step up onto the box and stand there a moment. With a small foal it's easy; just guide them to the box, give a little push, and they quickly hop on. Once up there, I give them lots of praise and reward them by scratching all their itchy spots. Young foals normally don't like to eat treats yet, so the itching is reward enough. The foals catch onto the idea very quickly and seem to enjoy it.

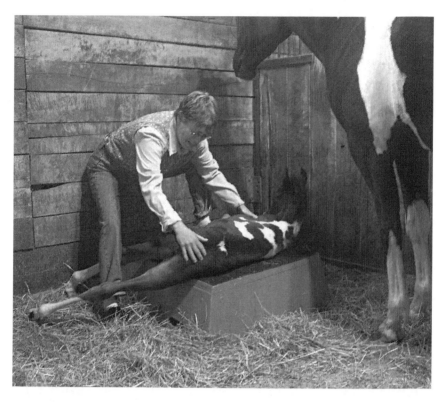

However, Darken was sure that the box was a colt-eating monster. Despite my gentle pushes, he wasn't getting anywhere near that thing. Finally, as I pushed and pushed, he launched toward it and landed, flat on his side, on top of the box. Not a very good beginning for a trick horse. After several more attempts, he stood on the box. Much to my chagrin, it made his legs look even more crooked. I didn't worry; he just needed more time to grow.

Some colts are naturally friendly, happy-go-lucky types that will walk right up to you for pets and scratches. Some colts are shy and hide behind their mothers, making them hard to catch. Some are adventurous and make their mothers chase after them as they race around the pasture looking for new things to explore. Darken was a timid scaredy-cat. Timid colts lack courage and self-confidence; they are nervous and tense, even when there is no reason. Every little noise or movement frightens them. Anything that alerts their senses is cause for alarm, then flight. Boy, did I pick the wrong colt to keep for myself.

One day my neighbor called to say her horses were sick and she wanted me to look at them. Their symptoms looked like strangles, a contagious disease that can make horses very sick. Later that day, her veterinarian confirmed our fears; they did indeed have strangles. The following day, I found Darken in this stall soaking wet from sweat. His mother seemed to be fine, but, with a temperature of 105 degrees, his entire little body was steaming. Although I had been careful to change my boots and clothes after being around my neighbor's sick horses, I was afraid that I had brought strangles into my barn. Turned out he had a mystery ailment that only lasted a few days and he quickly recovered. That was the first of the medical scares he would give me.

As Darken continued to grow, he filled out and became a hand-some colt. His coat was blacker than black, making his white spots seem to jump off his body. My farrier, Bill, made regular visits to trim Darken's hooves. His legs and tendons had improved a lot. He now walked on the bottoms of his hooves, instead of on the backs of his pasterns. His legs certainly appeared to be in perfect working order and he made good use of them. He could make the air whistle when he kicked and bucked in the pasture.

I pride myself that my horses are so well trained. They could always be counted on to be obedient and quiet. Bill would occasionally tell stories about some of the bad-mannered horses he had to work with and we'd laugh. I wasn't laughing anymore, because I now had one of those colts. Once, while holding Darken for Bill, I coughed. The unexpected noise scared Darken so badly that I thought he was going to come out of his skin. Despite hours of working with him, each time was a struggle to keep him still for Bill to pick up his feet long enough to get them trimmed. Even while his feet were being trimmed, Darken's attention always seemed to be somewhere else. It wasn't the act of trimming his hooves that worried him, but something as simple as the noise of one of Bill's metal tools being set down on the concrete floor. Any sudden movement or noise would make him pull his legs away, causing Bill's face to turn red from suppressing a bad word or two. Darken didn't mind that his legs were being handled, but if there was suddenly a danger he needed to run from, he knew he would need all four of his feet on the ground.

Despite struggling with Darken to quit fidgeting, Bill, who didn't have a lot of patience for silliness, liked this colt. I think Bill would have liked him even more if the horse lived in another state. Bill would say things like, "When this colt grows up, you're going to be able to sell him for a lot of money." The emphasis was always on "when you sell him". Still, coming from him, I took that as a compliment. Darken was certainly not a good example of my training skills and he was a bit of an embarrassment. I had no explanation for why he acted the way he did and why he really wasn't getting any better. He was supposed to be my star student.

On more than one occasion, I am sure Bill questioned why I would keep such a squirrelly colt. Clearly, he had little future either as a show horse or a trick horse. He might not even be safe enough to just trail ride. Darken was never a mean colt, just very sensitive, easily distracted, and easily startled. He was always happy to see me and he never once tried to bite or kick. It was just that his clock spring was wound a little too tight; his batteries were always fully charged, and everything he did was at full throttle. In his attempt to flee from a scary movement or noise, he just might accidentally flatten you on his way out of town. I hoped that with maturity, experience, and training, he would become easier to handle, but I was beginning to doubt that I could help him.

Every day I continued to work with Darken, trying to help him overcome his fear of the world. I spent lots of quiet time just brushing him and trying to gain his trust. When he was weaned, we built him a new stall in the indoor arena where he could see all the comings and goings of the barn. From his stall, he was able to watch the other horses in training. He was right in the middle of all the action and I hoped that he'd learn to be more confident and brave. He didn't. Even though his mother's stall was right next to his, he spent his first few days trying to get out of it. He'd stand on his hind legs trying to get his head and front legs over its seven foot walls. If something startled him, such as someone quickly opening the barn door, he'd bounce off all four walls like a ball in a pinball machine. Yet, things such as clipping his ears, which often unnerves the calmest of horses, didn't cause him the least bit of concern. He was perplexing to say the least.

Arabians are one of the most sensitive breeds. In their native land, Arabians were highly prized for this sensitivity. At night, the master often took his favorite mare into his tent. Alert to all movement, sights, and smells, her actions would warn her master of any danger long before her master would sense it himself. Their legendary stamina makes them the endurance horse of choice, and their beauty and intelligence is second to none. This sensitivity causes Arabians to respond to subtle cues, which also makes them my breed of choice for trick training.

Darken was just doing what his ancestors were bred for centuries to do and he took his job very seriously. His eyes and ears were especially sharp and they didn't miss a thing. He alerted me to the odd leaf blowing, the neighbor's cat in the yard, and a whole host of scary looking shadows and bushes that surely had trolls lurking behind them. I was constantly made well aware of the many dangers that surrounded us. Unfortunately, most of his actions seemed more like self-preservation, rather than warnings. He was always true to himself, acting exactly like a sensitive horse should. It was only when I wanted him to be something else that we had problems.

One day, while I was standing beside him in his stall, he backed his rear leg into his water bucket. The touch and sound scared him and caused him to race around inside his stall like a rocket. His chest hit me squarely in the back, instantly squishing me, like a bug, into one of the walls. I wasn't hurt, but I was caught off guard by his sensitivity to something as common as the touch of a bucket. This was a lesson I should have taken more seriously; Darken's fear of buckets would come back to haunt me in the future.

Unexpected sounds or movement were always cause for concern. He over-reacted to the slightest sounds or touches, causing him to blunder into things in his attempt to escape. He would frantically run away, and then look suspiciously back over his shoulder to see what had startled him. Better safe than sorry was his motto. Always hopeful, I assumed he would become more confident with time and training. After all, he was only a weanling; maybe I was expecting too much of him. However, none of my other weanlings ever over-reacted like he did. They seemed to take everything new in stride and with great interest.

Soon, Darken was a yearling and was joined by a new black and white pinto baby sister. We named her Dancin. She would grow up to be a very talented trick horse, winner of many championships, and Darken's best equine friend.

Thoughts of Darken ever becoming a trick horse were beginning to seem out of the question. He was so tense and afraid of everything; I gave up trying to teach him even a few simple tricks and spent all my time trying to teach him to be just a normal horse. The problem was he didn't want to be normal. Being silly was much more fun. Clever and constantly busy, he worked at things until he figured them out.

Darken's stall contained a feed door in one corner that was held shut with a metal latch. It wasn't long until he figured out how to unlatch it so he could hang his head out the door. He could unlatch it faster than I could latch it. The moment I'd turn my back, he'd flip the latch and fling the door open with his nose. He delighted in it. I'd whip around and catch him with the door open, his head hanging out with a smile on his face. I was afraid that if something spooked him enough he might attempt jumping out that little open door, or worse, get half way out and get stuck. I had to keep it secured with a chain; that made him very unhappy. Even with a chain on the door, if he worked at it long enough, he was still able to open it occasionally. I'd find him in the morning with his head hanging out the door and everything within reach played with.

In another attempt to help him learn to settle down, I'd often turn him loose in the barn to browse around on his own while I worked there. Darken loved it. He'd streak out of his stall to the indoor arena, zip out the door to the stable, and then fly down the barn aisle to visit one particular horse. As soon as Darken was loose, he'd make a beeline straight for the stall of an older gelding named Tysn. Darken knew exactly where he wanted to go the moment his stall door opened and he couldn't wait to get there. I'd catch sight of the end of his black tail as it disappeared around the corner. He delighted in annoying Tysn, whose stall was around the corner and at the far end of the barn. He'd trot down the aisle, ignoring a line of horses hanging their heads over the stall doors; the young horses wanted him to stay and play while the broodmares all tried to snap at him as he passed, heading straight to Tysn's stall.

There, over the half door, he'd play "nippy face" with Tysn, as if they were sword fighting with their noses. Tysn sometimes seemed to enjoy his visits, but most of the time he'd slyly try to maneuver Darken into a position where he could give him a good bite on the back of his neck. Darken seemed oblivious to Tysn's warning signs of flattened ears and threatening teeth, and just wanted to play. Poor Tysn spent a lot of time just wishing this annoying colt would go away, yet he always put his head over his stall door so Darken could reach him. I wondered what would happen when they finally were pastured together. I worried that Tysn would finally have the chance to flatten Darken, since Tysn considered himself "King of the Pasture", as well as the barn.

All colts like to cavort in the barn when they are loose. They take things off the shelves and play with them, but I've never had a colt that planned it as gleefully as Darken did. He reveled in his "barn tours". If there were things on the shelves, he would knock them all off. It was his passion. I'd catch a glimpse of him flashing by with something in his mouth and I'd have to track him down to remove a broom, a brush, or a feed scoop from his teeth. Off he'd run to find something else to play with. Sometimes he'd grab my coat or a towel and dash off with it. Suddenly, he'd notice that it was flapping in the wind and scary looking. Rather than dropping it, he'd clench his teeth tighter in fear and race around, the item seeming to chase after him. Eventually, he'd drop it. A few minutes later, I'd hear a ripping sound and go to investigate. I'd find him standing on the offending item and ripping it apart with his teeth, just for the fun of it. The coat, towel, or empty feed bag that a few minutes ago was a terrifying monster, was now a play toy to be ripped to shreds. Maybe I shouldn't have let him loose like that, but he had such fun, I just couldn't resist. Besides, I had a reason; if he could roam and investigate at his own pace, possibly he'd learn that the world was not such a scary place.

The idea seemed to be helping him, and he had such a wonderful time getting into everything, though still under my watchful eye. He was always such a puzzlement, yet fun to watch. A ray of light shining through a crack in the barn siding and onto the floor would cause him to bow up his neck, lower his head to get a good look, snort, then leap away from it like it was alive. Yet, he could weave himself through a tight maze of buggies and carts parked in the aisle without an ounce of concern. Whenever he was loose, if I was working intently on a project, a fuzzy black nose would silently glide in over my shoulder and get between my face and my project. I am sure he thought he was helping. When I was done with chores or had had enough of his antics, I'd tell him to get back to his stall and he'd make a dash for it. When I got to his stall to shut the door, he'd be standing there, peering down at his feed dish, looking innocent and expecting dinner.

Although he was often a frustration, he did have a way of making me smile. With each leap, spin, or free-for-all dash around the indoor arena, I couldn't help but admire how easily and gracefully he moved. I also couldn't help but wonder, with moves like that, how I was ever going to stay in his saddle.

Whenever anyone came to look at young horses for sale, they were always drawn to Darken's stall and wanted to buy him. Each time I said no, mostly because I knew he was too much horse for most people to safely handle. According to my long-suffering, non-horsey husband, I had too many horses. I did need to sell a few, but I wanted to keep Darken for myself. When there are bills to pay and a buyer makes an offer, you are always tempted to accept. However, I found myself quickly ushering people past his stall to look at other colts and fillies that were quieter and would be easier to train. It would have been easier for me to have kept one or two of the quieter ones, but like everyone else, I was drawn to that striking "little black fox".

One day, a man and his family came to look at a filly I had for sale. They were browsing around, peeking into each stall, then from across the barn I heard, "Is the one with the postage stamp spot for sale?" The man had a young family and I knew Darken would not be a good match with young children. Again I said no, and as soon as I did the adrenaline rush in my stomach went away; yes he was proving to be impossible, but I still wanted to keep Darken for myself. I showed the family a gentle, easy-going filly and they immediately fell in love with her and took her home. I still get Christmas photo cards from the family with the filly wearing a Santa hat standing next to their smiling children. They had made a wise choice.

Chapter 4

THE BUCKET DISASTER

WHEN DARKEN was two years old, I thought it was time to sit on his back, just for a minute. I am a strong believer that horses should not be seriously ridden until they are at least three years old; four is even better. Too many people are in such a hurry to get their youngsters under saddle, that they risk damage to their colt's still-growing joints, which can shorten their useful lives. I had no desire to push or rush Darken and I would not take any chance of hurting him. I had plenty of other horses to ride while waiting until Darken was old enough to be started under saddle. I just wanted to see what it felt like to sit on him. You can tell a lot about a horse just by quietly sitting on his back. It can give you advance notice about how the colt will react when it does come time to train him to ride. Will he be nervous or take everything in stride?

I had already driven Darken in long lines, walking behind him, and he was getting pretty good at steering around. He understood how to turn in different directions, stop, and back up. He seemed to accept the idea pretty well, so I thought he was ready for the next step. I was wrong. I slipped the bit into his mouth, slid the bridle up and over his pretty face, and crossed the reins over his neck. Because I was afraid to sit on him loose in the large arena, I chose the relative safety of his small, enclosed box stall. To get on his bare back, I thought it would be a good idea to stand on an overturned bucket. I got up on the bucket and jumped up onto his back.

He had really grown a lot. I quietly sat there admiring his little black ears sticking up a few inches out of a tangle of now long black mane. He looked a lot bigger from the vantage point of his back. His neck was remarkably thicker with a mass of muscle I hadn't noticed before. I had not seen him from this angle since he was a newborn foal lying sprawled across my lap.

All was well until he took a step forward and kicked the bucket with a rear hoof. The noise and movement of the bucket caused him to rocket forward in a blind panic. The more he ran, the harder he'd kick the bucket that was now being knocked around under his feet. He raced around and around inside his stall with me clinging to his back. He'd stop for a moment, try to climb up the walls, and then bolt off again around and around and around, with no sign of slowing down. I wanted off but was afraid I'd be trampled if I tried. I had to pick my moment to jump and pick it quickly. When it became clear that I had to get off before I was thrown off, I leaped off and promptly got knocked down, as his chest hit me from behind. Ducking under his corner feeder was the only thing that saved me.

Never again would I mount spooky colts from empty buckets in a stall, that's for sure. It was entirely my fault for doing such a stupid thing and I did not blame poor Darken for his reaction. But now the seed of doubt was planted. Was I ever going to be able to ride him? He was too wild for others; now he seemed too wild for me. I was heartbroken.

Not only was it likely that Darken would never become a trick horse, but now it seemed he was a poor choice as a show horse. Timid horses usually do not make good competition horses. Their lack of self-confidence makes them tense and erratic under saddle. There are times of brilliance, when they seem to hold it all together, but they are easily distracted and it's a constant struggle to keep them focused. Meltdowns and panic attacks are a common occurrence when their senses become overloaded with new sights and sounds. Darken certainly wasn't a good choice to become my star pupil.

As I pondered on how I was ever going to ride this colt, I remembered a small black pup I brought home one day many years before. It was another one of those events in my life that I remember so clearly. While simple and innocent at the time, it ended up having a profound effect on me, a turning point in my life that I can pinpoint to the day. I walked to school every day since my elementary school was within sight of my home. One day, on the way home, a neighbor invited me in to look at their free puppies. She didn't have to ask me twice. The mother dog was a big, black, hairy creature which looked to have some Collie blood in her somewhere. A bunch of black puppies with tan legs squirmed beside her as she lay in an old tool shed behind the house. They all looked the same, except for a few with white toes or a white tip on the end of their tails. Of course, I wanted one in the worst way. I rushed home and asked my parents, who were not amused. They weren't really against the idea of me having a puppy, just not one from that mamma dog. Her pups grew up to be no good. My grandmother had nothing good to say about our neighbor's no-good dogs either. She disliked them even more than my parents did, probably because they frequently ate her chickens. That didn't stop me; I nagged and whined until they finally relented.

The next day on my way home from school I stopped in and picked out a pup. I spent a long time deciding which one was *the* one and settled on one with both white toes and a white tip on the end of his tail. My uncle later scared me to death when he offered to cut that white tip off with his jackknife, but he was only joking. I named the pup Hector. I was determined that I could overcome the odds and train him to be good. He turned out to be an amazing dog.

Many years later, my grandmother was picking apples way out back in the orchard when she fell out of a tree and broke her leg. She didn't want anyone to know she had done such a foolish thing at her age, so she tried crawling home, but didn't get far. She gave up and called for help. The first to arrive and the one who would sit with her until the ambulance arrived was Hector. He might have been the only good dog his mother ever produced, but even grandma had to admit—he was a good one. That one little pup started a flame that still burns in me today. I love taking problem animals that need a little extra work and help them develop into champions, if not in the show ring, at least in their owners' hearts.

Over the years, I have bought, trained, and found new homes for quite a few problem or abused horses. They were often horses sent to auction only because of behavioral issues. None were really mean or dangerous; usually they were just spoiled or allowed to become disrespectful of their owners. Consistent training, gentle handling, and finding them a job they enjoyed usually turned them around within a few months, and then I could find them new homes.

I really enjoyed working with these types of horses and they taught me a lot. In addition to basic training, teaching them how to perform a few tricks went a long way toward gaining their trust. It also gave them a way to earn praise. It was often the perfect thing they needed and helped open the door to their willingness to learn. They quickly learned there was something to be gained by paying attention. In this way, the horse becomes more responsive to your other commands as well.

I put everything I learned from them into Darken, but he was so different from any other horse I had ever trained. He was a happy horse, respectful, and most certainly never abused. He didn't really have an excuse for being the way he was. I couldn't quite put my finger on what he needed.

It would have been too easy to point a finger at his parents and try to lay the blame on them. Some bloodlines are a little hotter than others, but again, Darken had no excuse there. Both his parents were wonderful horses. His sire was well known for his easily trainable offspring and many had gone on to become show champions. Darken's mother was practically a saint.

Like my pup Hector, blame could not be placed on his parents. In the pup's case, his siblings earned their bad reputation from their irresponsible owner who gave them no training and let them run wild, getting into trouble wherever they found it. Darken didn't have the excuse of an irresponsible owner and no training. All the training methods that had worked on my other horses, were not working on him, and I had no idea why not. I'd spent many hours quietly working with him, giving him lots of turn out play time, and I even tried adjusting his diet. Occasionally I'd try to get him to step up onto the box again and stand there a moment, but his attention was always somewhere else. I never had a horse that trick training didn't help, yet Darken failed at that too.

No, Darken simply had a personality all his own. Quirky, timid, funny, alert, alive, bouncy, happy, willing, silly… the list was endless. If I could just figure out what made him tick, I might find a better way to understand him and find a training method for him. Then, he and I would be able to conquer the world. At least we might be able to enjoy a trail ride or someday make it into a show ring together.

While all my young horses were individuals with slight variances in intelligence and talent, I found most of them remarkably easy to train, especially to teach tricks. With the troubles I was having with Darken, I found I was becoming more interested in the journey rather than hurrying to achieve the end result. While I enjoyed having a goal, achieving it quickly wasn't so important anymore. His poor progress did frustrate me at times, but I found him fascinating.

Rather than take the easy way out with Darken and selling him, my new plan was to enjoy and savor each step along the way. I didn't want to be in such a hurry that I missed the little things that happen each day, that often get ignored in our hurry to get someplace else. I was going to do his training slowly and I was going to do it right. I was not going to force or rush him. I also had no intention of babying him to the point of allowing him to become a useless and dangerous pet. He would be expected to learn a job and do it well.

The best thing any owner can do for their horse, besides taking proper care of it, is teaching it a useful skill. I was going to put all the knowledge and skills I had gained in my forty years of training into this colt. And, in the end, I expected to be rewarded with a champion. Little did I know how many steps it was going to take.

Chapter 5

SPOTTY

DARKEN'S MOTHER, Spotty, was a perfect example of a wonderful horse whose only flaw was being spoiled by her owner. I bought her when she was just five months old but she had already learned a bad habit. When I tried to load her into my trailer to bring her home, she fell down. I thought it was an accident and that she'd slipped on the paved driveway. Once home, I quickly found out that anytime she didn't get her way, she threw herself down on the ground. She wasn't mean, just a bit spoiled.

Being a trick horse trainer, it was only natural that I would immediately start teaching Spotty a few simple tricks to try to overcome her bad habit. Not only is trick training a wonderful way to develop a close bond of trust with a horse, but it teaches horses to be more responsive, confident, and happy performers in any discipline.

The first time I led her up to the wooden box to teach her to stand on it, down she went. She'd look at it a moment, rear up, turn in mid air, and throw herself on the ground, knocking the breath out of herself. That dangerous behavior wasn't going to work at *my* barn. She quickly learned that throwing herself on the ground didn't work; she still had to do what she didn't want to do. I'd walk her up to the box, she'd throw herself down, and I'd wait until she got up and walk her up to the box again. After a few repeats, she gave up and stepped up onto the box and was immediately rewarded with lots of praise. Once she understood that praise would always follow the correct response, she went on to become a remarkable horse with a gentle and kind soul.

Spotty learned many tricks, including one of the most difficult for a trick horse; sitting flat on the ground from a standing position. Nearly all horses can sit down on something, such as a bale of hay or specially built platform or chair that is strong enough to support their weight, yet soft enough not to rub their hocks. Trick horses will back up until they feel the security of something behind them; then they feel safe enough to lower themselves down onto it. Few horses are willing to sit down flat on the ground from a standing position, because it involves a great deal of trust that the ground will be there. A horse's vision is such that there is a blind spot directly behind them. When you ask a horse to sit, it is as if you are asking him to sit down into an unknown space. Sitting down turned out to be Spotty's specialty. She gladly demonstrated this special ability to the countless children who came to see her.

When it came time to train her to ride, I worried that she might remember her old habit of throwing herself down when things didn't go her way. I worried she might throw herself over backwards on top of me, so I put a lot of extra training time into her before I hopped on her back and asked her to take a few steps. She tossed her head and I could feel her front feet lift off the ground just a bit. This was the pivotal moment; she'd either rear or go forward. I held my breath, squeezed her with my legs, and she walked forward. She never made another misstep. On her third ride, I took her out trail riding. She was that easy and I expected her son to be just like her.

We loved Spotty for six years, but one day she just wasn't herself. After many vet visits, treatments, and medications, not to mention a whopping vet bill, she lay down in her stall at the vet clinic, took her last breath, and quietly passed away from pneumonia.

I knew she was sick, but when the phone call came that she had passed away, it caught me completely off guard. I had not even considered for a moment that she might actually die from her illness. I took her to the vet clinic to be cured and I fully expected nothing less. My heart was crushed. Up until this point, Spotty was the best horse I'd ever owned—perfect in body, mind, and soul. She was everything I could have wished for in a horse. She was young and had so much untapped potential. She was also my friend and I was heartbroken. All those great plans I had made for her were now going to be unfulfilled. Life is often not what we plan or assume. Spotty was gone, and so was what I thought would be my easy ticket to the winner's circle.

We brought her home and buried her under our kitchen window with one of her championship ribbons around her neck. We wanted her close so we could talk to her every day. The only thing that helped ease my heart was the knowledge that I had done everything that I and veterinary science could do to try to save her. It was unthinkable that my beautiful and gentle Spotty was actually gone.

A wise old veterinarian once said, "If you have livestock, you are going to have dead stock." It's true that even with the best of care, things happen you can't control. Like most animal-loving families, we have a little pet cemetery in the corner of our yard where our faithful dog and cat friends, who'd shared their lives with us, lay buried.

Spotty left behind her two offspring, Darken, now two, and his full sister, Dancin, a yearling. Spotty lives within each of them and I would do my best to honor her by helping them reach their full potential. I would see where they led me next.

Chapter 6

THE ACCIDENT

I DIDN'T have long to wait for my next adventure. It lead me straight back to the site of my last adventure, and it wasn't good.

Four days after his mother's passing, Darken and I had one of our usual morning work sessions together. He was learning many new things, but he was still so skittish that every day was a challenge. A few hours later, I went back out to the barn to clean his stall, only to find him with a thin trickle of fresh blood running out of his right nostril. After a quick search, I found a small hole the size of a pencil eraser in his forehead. It looked as if he'd been neatly shot with a .22 bullet. Since it was unlikely that he could have been shot inside the barn, he must have run his head into something like a bolt or nail. Although we covered every inch of his stall, we never found anything that could have caused the injury. Talk about a horse needing a padded stall!

A quick call to the veterinarian resulted in me hauling him to the same equine clinic where his mother had recently died. It was the first time that Darken had been hauled any distance, but he traveled pretty well. I pulled around to the back of the clinic where the big overhead garage doors were located. I rang their door bell to alert the staff that I had arrived. A staff member came to the door and pressed another button to lift the huge metal garage door. Up it went in a smooth, industrial sounding way, much the way I assume the doors would sound at a slaughter house. Darken must have had the same thought on his mind as he watched the big doors go up, revealing a large, dark, medical-smelling interior.

I nearly panicked when they told me to bring him inside, but it had to be done. Darken tentatively tiptoed behind me, down the cement aisle, while glancing left and right at the rows of stalls. We had entered the clinic through the horse barn part of the building. It was huge with large stalls on both sides of the aisle. Most of the horses temporarily stabled there for treatment were towering giants of horseflesh, most likely race horses. Most stood like statues in their stalls, in bandages, or hooked up to IVs, calmly munching hay, seemingly without a care in the world. There were also a few mares with sick newborn foals lying beside them that glared at anyone who dared look through the stall bars at their babies. For someone such as me, who loves the equine medical field, it smelled like a wonderful combination of horses, straw, disinfectant, and iodine, a medical smell that sticks on you long after you go home. To Darken, it was a terrible smell of the unknown, strangers, confinement, medications, needles, and death.

Once inside the building, we were ushered toward a large, clean exam room. My scaredy-cat colt was going to have to walk into a huge room filled with expensive medical equipment and rolling trays of fragile looking instruments. They had to be kidding! Just the sound of the overhead door opening and closing in his face was enough to cause him to panic and skitter around with bugged out eyes. The problem was solved by giving him a sedation shot that made him sleepy. As the medication took effect, he stood with his head lowered, his legs braced apart to keep his balance, and his nose pressed against my stomach. As I felt his warm breath blowing softly through the weave of my shirt, I wished that he could relax like that at home. How nice it would be if he didn't have to be concerned with every bird that flew through the barn or overreact every time a door slammed. How much easier he would be to handle and maybe even ride someday, if he could just relax. I wish I could have told him that he didn't need to be so fearful all the time. He would still be safe if he could just let his guard down a little. He could trust me and I would do my best to take care of him. However, it's hard to get a horse to trust and believe in people after bringing him to such a scary place and allowing strangers to stick him with needles.

An x-ray revealed broken bits of bone around the hole in his forehead. The x-ray could not tell for sure what else might be damaged, so they scheduled him for a CAT scan. I would have to leave him at the clinic. We had never before been parted overnight. I felt as if I was leaving my injured child at the hospital. How would he manage without me, his only mother, since his real mother had just passed away? Would he be afraid, would he be good for them, would they be good to him? Not only had I closely lived with him for the past two years, but I had seen him on an ultrasound machine fifteen days after his conception, when he was nothing more than a few dividing cells. The drive home with an empty trailer was very lonely.

For his CAT scan, he had to have more medication that caused him to go into a deep sleep so he could be put onto a rolling table and have his head put into the machine. A CAT scan machine is a large donut-shaped machine that would take x-ray images at many different angles around his head. The images would then be processed by a computer to produce cross-sectional pictures of the internal structure of his skull. It was a good thing that he was asleep, as just the sight of that machine would have caused him sheer terror. Thankfully, he remained in a drug-induced sleep for the whole procedure and didn't wake up until he was safely back in his stall in the clinic barn.

The scan revealed that he had fractured his skull, but the damage was limited to only the bones at the top of his sinuses. Had the damage been slightly higher, it would have gone into the base of his brain and he would have been given a poor prognosis—a very poor prognosis. He would need surgery to fix the broken bones in his forehead and then receive repeated sinus flushings for a few days. I warned the stable girls, who would be taking care of him, that he was very skittish and that they needed to be very careful around him. I warned them never to touch his legs unexpectedly.

They seemed to brush me off, not really paying much attention. They probably thought I was an overly concerned owner, but I needed to impress upon them that I was serious. This horse could hurt them if they weren't careful. He was not like the typical cranky race horses in their care who might take a snarly bite or random kick at them. Darken was dangerous because, if something scared him, he would overreact before he thought about what he was doing. He might kick or knock them down, not from meanness, but from fear, especially in a strange barn. I am sure they handled a lot of troublemakers and knew how to deal with them safely. Most of the horses taken to their clinic came from the race track; horses not well known for being easy to handle. The girls didn't seem very concerned about my pony-sized, two year old colt and said he would be fine, but I knew that they'd just give him more drugs if he gave them any trouble.

When I went to visit him the following day, it was odd to see the warning sign "STALLION" hanging on his stall door. I hadn't really thought of my screwball colt as a stallion. He certainly wasn't yet aware of being a full fledged stallion. The mares at home found him annoying and flattened their ears and made ugly faces at him over the fence. I thought it funny the clinic should post a warning to the stable girls that he was a stallion, when it was his school girl skittishness that was the real danger.

Four days later, I was able to bring him home. I was given a substantial bill and a DVD of his CAT scan. The DVD was very detailed, allowing me to even see the folds of his brain. Now, I had proof that he actually did have a brain. Until then, I had pictured his brain looking much like confetti in the wind—scattered everywhere. He came home with his head wrapped up like a mummy, with only his eyes, ears, and nose sticking out. Under the wrap, he had a dozen purple stitches in his forehead. He seemed very glad when the day finally came that I could take off his protective wrappings. I worried that he would re-injure himself and send us back to the clinic again, but his recovery was pleasantly uneventful.

As a result of the fracture, he was left with a thumbprint-sized permanent dent in his forehead, just below his star. Around the dent is a starburst of white hairs that grew in where the stitches had been. That dent would one day become a place where countless children would place their thumbs.

Chapter 7

INTO THE SHOW RING

ONE MONTH later was the entry deadline for the Pinto World Championship show in Tulsa, Oklahoma; a month after that, the actual show. Up to this point, Darken had never stepped hoof into a show ring. I should probably not have considered entering him since he was still so squirrelly, but the show offered a class for two year old colts and I felt he deserved a shot at it. His mother had won her two year old class there, and wouldn't it be grand if her son could do the same, in her memory? I had two months to get him ready. His surgery site had healed, the vet said he was fit to go to the show, and he was back to his usual playful antics that kept the barn in a constant uproar.

Darken was still too young to be ridden, so the plan would be to only show him in-hand at halter. At the world show, halter horses are hand-led before three judges and are scored on their conformation and movement. Darken had grown into a strikingly good looking colt and he had an unmistakable charisma about him that always turned heads. We would go.

He had been in a trailer for short trips to the vet clinic, but Tulsa was a long way from northeastern Ohio. I sent in his entry, but the thought of hauling a skittish colt that far, by myself, was a little daunting. It would be an adventure, for sure.

In preparation for the world show, Darken needed to go to some smaller local shows for practice. It would be a good chance for him to get some show ring experience under his belt and to build his confidence. How hard could it be? The plan was to take him and just lead him around the show grounds to take in all the sights and sounds. I'd hauled lots of other colts and fillies to their first shows.

They were always nervous in the beginning, whinnying and dancing around at the excitement of being in a new place. However, they'd quickly relax and look at the shows as fun places to go with exciting new things to see and do.

When I pulled into the show grounds for the first time with Darken, I could feel by the way he was furiously pawing and rocking the horse trailer that he was going to be different. Cautiously, I unloaded a frazzled and sweaty Darken. He was a coiled spring, ready to launch in any direction, including on top of my head. It had taken so long at home to give him a bath, that by the time we arrived at the grounds, all the stalls had been filled. I knew he wouldn't stand tied to the trailer without twirling around and tangling himself up in his tie rope. For safety sake, he would stay inside his trailer when not being walked around the grounds. Everyone knew which trailer was mine, as there was a steady sound of hoof beats coming from it. I spent those first few shows just trying to hang onto him. I hoped that when he learned that things weren't going to hurt him, he'd relax and enjoy the show. If he would just trust me, things would be alright.

However, his brain told him that to be safe; he needed to keep his feet and body in constant motion. He'd jump away from other horses, shy away from running children; just the sight of grates over the storm drains was cause for great alarm. At home, we had no barking dogs or noisy children, so he had no prior experience with them. Until now, he had only known his quiet pasture, his barn, his stable mates, and his stall. The horse show was a big adjustment with scary surprises for him around every corner.

When something startled him, he would quickly spread his front feet, mash my toes, and then squat down in preparation to leap off my foot in one direction or another. I got pretty good at guessing which way he'd jump, thus saving my toes from yet another stomping. He nearly knocked me down in an attempt to avoid several laughing girls. When we passed a group of exhibitors brushing their sleepy-looking horses, they said how pretty he was. I was getting dragged along so I didn't have long to stay and chat. I jokingly asked if they'd like to lead him and they answered back in unison, "NO". He was pretty to look at, but far too scary for them to ever want to handle themselves. While Darken was proving to be a handful at the shows, it was clear that he just had sensory overload. There were so many unfamiliar horses and distractions to capture his attention that keeping him calm and focused on me seemed like an impossible task. Gentle handling, time, and experience would hopefully teach him that he had nothing to fear.

As hoped, he got a little better at each show and, eventually, I was able to actually get him into the show ring. Little by little, I was able to leave him tied to the trailer for short periods and was eventually able to leave him in a stall. Although I still didn't trust him enough to be able to leave the top half of his stall door open so he could hang his head out, he was showing a lot of improvement. The many hours I spent working with him were beginning to pay off and he began winning ribbons. He ended the show season winning the year-end high point award for his division. One of his awards was a black halter and lead with his name embroidered on it in neon pink lettering. Not a very manly color for a stallion. Perhaps word had gotten out about how chicken he really was.

Chapter 8

THE JOURNEY

IN JUNE, Darken and I made the long trip to Tulsa, Oklahoma. Since it was a three day trip for us, we stayed overnight at fairgrounds along the way. The fairgrounds were usually empty, except for the harness racing horses that live and train there. The fairground gates would all be locked, except for the one gate closest to the horse barns. They were open so the race horse owners could care for and train their horses. I can usually slip in this open gate and park somewhere inside for the night. It's far safer when traveling alone than a truck stop. It also enables me to unload my horse so I can walk him around to stretch his legs a bit away from traffic.

One night we had the good fortune to stay at a fairground which was hosting a high school rodeo. As I looked around the stables, the tacked up stock horses looked very relaxed and happy in their stalls, waiting for their next event. They all hung their heads over the low stall walls into their neighboring horse's stall. The staff there offered me a stall for Darken for the night, but the stalls were so flimsy that I didn't trust Darken to keep his nose and teeth to himself. I knew he would spend his time chewing up the saddle on any horse stalled next to him. I turned him loose in my trailer, which was like a big box stall inside, where he'd be safer for the night. In the morning I found that he'd kept himself entertained all night by ripping the trailer padding to shreds.

The following night, I stayed at an empty fairground. Since the fairgrounds were quiet and it was stifling hot, I decided to try tying Darken to the outside of the trailer all night, something I'd never done before. He seemed happy, pulling mouthfuls of hay from his hay bag. It was so muggy inside my trailer that I slept outside on the ground beside my truck, on a blanket spread over the cool grass. That way, I could also keep an ear open to what Darken was doing, in case he got into trouble.

In the middle of the night, a heavy fog rolled in and hung in the air four feet off the ground. I awoke to Darken's alarm snorts. These were not little "I see something sneaking up on me!" snorts, but the hair-raising alarm blasts that horses do through their nostrils to warn other horse to "RUN FOR YOUR LIVES!" At home, that sound was reserved for crisp fall mornings when he'd stop running in the pasture, lift his head, and let out a huge blowing blast through his nose. His tail would be flung over his back and he'd turn and run a few laps around the pasture before returning to his hay pile for breakfast.

This time, something was causing him to be more frightened than I had ever seen him before. He felt the need, not only to save himself, but to wake the whole neighborhood and warn them, too. Alone hundreds of miles from home, whatever was scaring him, was scaring me, too. For once, his warning was something I needed to heed. In the pitch darkness and fog, I could see truck lights across the grassy lot where I was parked. Out of those lights came black things walking toward us. Poor Darken was panicked and pulling on his tie rope for all he was worth.

The approaching things were black cows. Turned out, that there was a Black Angus beef show there the following day and people were beginning to arrive with their cattle, late at night, the evening before the show. They were unloading their stock and walking them toward the barns through the fog. In my pajamas and bare feet, I untied Darken before he broke loose, which was seconds away, and put him back inside the trailer. Very uncharacteristically, I never heard another peep out of him the rest of the night. No fussing around, no pawing, just silence. He was trying to be very quiet and hide from the cows so they wouldn't find and eat him.

The next day we headed out; he seemed to be glad we were on our way again. Driving along the highway, I began to see billboard signs for the Roy Rogers and Dale Evans Museum in Branson, Missouri. Years ago the museum was in Victorville, California. I'd always wanted to see it, but it was too far from Ohio. When Branson became a bigger tourist attraction, the museum was moved to Missouri. I always wanted to see all of Roy's memorabilia and, of course, his horse Trigger, who was now mounted and on display there. We turned off the highway and headed the additional fifty-five miles to Branson.

Driving a horse trailer through downtown Branson is practically a thrill ride. The roads are twisty and tilted and there is tight parking everywhere. I had to stop and ask directions to the museum several times. It was surprising to me that no one had heard of it. We finally found the museum on the edge of town and right next to it was a nice little dirt parking lot; the only spare spot of dirt left in Branson in which to park a horse trailer. Darken was more than happy to stop for a rest. I got him a fresh bucket of water, filled up his hay bag, and he was set.

I had a great time touring the museum, especially seeing Trigger and the other mounted animals that were part of Roy's TV shows and movies. How ironic it was that I was there, with my horse waiting in the parking lot, to see the man and his horse that started me on the journey to owning my own trick horses.

I will always treasure the time I took to veer off the highway and go see Roy's museum. After operating for 45 years, it was soon to close and the collection to be dispersed in 2009. It is very sad that kids today haven't grown up with the old TV western cowboy stars like Gene Autry, Tex Ritter, and Hopalong Cassidy. Many, like Roy Rogers, were role models who encouraged kids to be courteous, brave but never take chances, respect their parents, clean their plates, study hard and learn all you can, go to Sunday School, say their prayers, take care of their pets, and much more.

Chapter 9

WORLD CHAMPIONSHIP

ONCE AT the Tulsa fairgrounds, the staff tried to assign Darken to a stall with a low-lying overhead electrical wire. Knowing my colt would have spent his entire time there trying to reach that wire with his teeth, so he could electrocute himself, I asked for a different stall. He got a stall fit for a king. Not only were there no electrical wires within reach, but its floor was covered in red carpet. The carpet was there to prevent the horses from slipping on the smooth cement, but it did lend an air of royalty to the place. I worried that he'd find a way to pull it up and choke on it, but surprisingly, he left it alone. Even the big PA speaker next to his stall never bothered him. He moved in and was quite content. I was pleasantly surprised. Maybe this was going to be easier than I thought. What a good horse.

I spent part of the evening scoping out my competition. One colt in particular had me worried. He was a big rose gray colt who was very mature looking for his age. Not only was he tall, but he was fit and well muscled. While he appeared very nice, he spent his time pacing around inside his stall and screaming until he'd worked himself into a white lather. For once, I didn't own the worst actor on the show grounds.

Since Darken had never been shown inside a huge indoor arena before, I expected the worst of him. It was crowded, noisy, and had more horses and people inside it than he'd seen in his whole life. The day before his class, I took him in several of the other indoor show rings for practice. Because the main show ring was always packed with dozens of exhibitors riding their horses and I was on foot, I practiced in several of the smaller and quieter show rings under the same roof. I even took him on a leisurely walk through all the barns to visit several of my friends. He walked amid scooters, golf carts, and the general chaos of a horse show without a care in the world. He was surprisingly calm, and I was thrilled with him. If he could handle that, he could handle anything, or so I thought.

The following day, we got ready for his class; I stood with him in the warm-up area waiting our turn to go into the main show ring. Darken was the picture of Arabian beauty with a coat that gleamed like silk. He had grown into a smooth-bodied colt with a long black mane and heavy thick tail. He moved in a slinky way with very loose and flexible joints. He moved much like a cat, able to effortlessly spring in any direction. I never had such a horse with so many good things going for him. If only I could just understand him better and help him overcome some of his silly behaviors.

Every hair was in place and his hooves were polished. He was responding well to my cues to stand up and strike his show pose. He was relaxed and happy, and I had a pocket full of his favorite treats to keep his attention. I took him as close as I could to the in-gate so he could get a good look inside the ring before his class. Several years earlier, my stallion, Black Tie, had entered this same ring and come out the winner of two high point trophy saddles. Now, here I was again, this time to prove Darken's worth. I couldn't wait to get him into the ring to show him off to the judges.

The main show ring was huge. There were banners hung over head and the announcer's voice boomed over the PA system. I didn't have any worries. Darken showed no fear of being inside the buildings. He didn't even seem to notice the loud PA speaker mounted just a few feet from his stall, and I'd walked him around the grounds until he seemed bored with the whole place. I did not get a chance to take him into the main show ring, but all the indoor rings were similar and he was calm in them. The only difference was that the main ring was much larger, air conditioned, and there were overhead seating areas on three sides. How much difference could that really make? The warm-up pen and the show ring were in the same building, separated by a cement block wall. Darken was practically asleep in the warm-up pen. We were ready to go.

Horses in the class preceding ours rushed out of the ring amid thunderous applause. Despite all the work I had done with Darken, to help him learn to handle his strong instincts when he felt pressured, he began to look worried. When he saw that horses were running, he thought there must be danger present. His head went up, his eyebrows wrinkled, and he tucked his tail between his hind legs at the noise and at the sudden flurry of excited people and horses around him. I reassured him, fed him a treat to distract him, took a breath, and lead him into the ring at a trot. We had come so far, worked so hard, and he had such a good chance at placing well; he could not fall apart now. All he had to do was what we'd practiced countless times—trot in, line up, strike his show pose, and stand still for inspection by the judges.

Once inside the show ring, he got one look at the overhead seating and people walking above him, and panicked. There were too many new things distracting him and he began to have a meltdown.

All his old fears were back. It didn't help that outside the ring it was a wilting 90 degrees and inside it was air-conditioned to a horsey "I feel good!" temperature.

It was all I could do to hang onto his show lead. Several times I seriously thought he would knock me down and get loose. He'd been a timid squirrel all his life, but this was the worst scene he'd ever made. He was not being mean, just scared out of his mind and I couldn't get his attention back on me. Finally I got him to stand still in the line up and then it happened. He started acting like he was going to lie down. He put both front feet out in front of himself and then tried to crouch down on his elbows. When all else had failed to get him out of that scary place, he thought maybe this would. It didn't. Perhaps, somewhere in the back of his mind, he had actually retained a bit of information from watching my trick horses practice. I had long ago given up teaching him any tricks and certainly hadn't taught him to lie down. I quickly got him back up standing on all four feet and looking like a show horse again. We made it through the class and I hoped that the three judges had missed his weird performance.

Despite it all, Darken was named the Reserve World Champion. They quickly handed me a silver belt buckle and a long ribbon as he was dragging me toward the out-gate. I hung onto his lead with one hand and hung on to his prizes with the other and tried not to run anyone over in the process. Once outside the ring, he heaved a huge sigh of relief, dropped his head, and calmly walked off like a petting zoo pony. On one side of the wall, he was terrified; on the other side of the wall, he wasn't. Lesson learned. At future shows, we would always practice in the main ring.

Chapter 10

THE PHOTO

BEFORE HEADING home, there was one last task to accomplish; posing for our "win" photo. We were not leaving without proper documentation of our win and proof of our accomplishment. While it sounds like an easy task, Darken always made everything a challenge. We took our place in a long, narrow, curtained alley amid a sea of other horses in line ahead of us, waiting to be photographed. Darken and I took our place at the end of the line and he began to look around at everything that was crammed into the little alley with us. All of the other horses were patiently waiting; some even appeared to be asleep. Their owners happily chitchatted with their entourage of family and friends, there to help them and be included in their photos.

Everyone else appeared to not have a care in the world. For them, it was an easy task to wait their turn, get their photo, and be on with their day. They stood in line with their awards, grooming bags, and an odd collection of chairs, snacks, and drinks they'd brought along for the long wait. Darken started off happy and relaxed and all was well, for a while.

As more horses took their place in line behind us and pushed us further into the alley, Darken became more worried. Since he was a stallion, I also had to worry about keeping our distance from other horses, but they kept crowding in tighter and tighter. In one hand I held Darken's lead, while he squirmed around on the other end of it. In my other hand, I held his two foot long slippery satin ribbon and trophy buckle in its big blue velvet case. Darken fidgeted, chewed on the end of his ribbon, and became more and more upset with the situation.

While the show ring was air-conditioned, the photographer's

area was not, so we began to get hot and sticky. I was running out of ways to keep Darken distracted and he was beginning to act like a two year old toddler having a meltdown in line at the grocery store.

To add to Darken's worry, we were surrounded on all sides by linen curtains, which billowed toward us with each rotation of a gigantic floor fan. Darken was sure that there was something sinister behind the walls of curtains, which, at any moment, was going to spring out and grab him by the ankles. He was not about to let that happen, so he kept his ankles moving. To move out of line, meant you moved to the back of the line and started all over again. We sure didn't want to do that and I really wanted that photo. We held our ground.

To make matters worse, the exhibitors ahead of us posed for photo after photo. Some wanted their families in their photos, some wanted their grandma or the grandkids, their trainer, even their dogs in the photo. All this took extra time and those of us in line were beginning to feel like hot sardines. Finally, it was our turn.

Thankfully, I was able to hand off our awards to someone; I was beginning to lose feeling in my hand from trying to hang onto them so long. Since there were two photographers, two horses were in the same small photo shoot area at the same time. I led Darken between two gigantic floor fans, two sets of expensive cameras set up on tripods at floor level, and through a tight maze of people, chairs, and other horses. We were instructed to stand on a strip of red carpet in front of a curtain backdrop, and behind a row of plastic stands on which our awards would sit. Darken was supposed to walk between them, set up in his show pose, and stand there long enough for his photo to be taken. Right!

Darken took one look at the curtain and all the decorations and would not get near them. After some convincing, he finally tiptoed across the carpet and into place. The photographer, being a perfectionist, insisted that Darken's feet be placed just so, which meant extra maneuvering. I was more worried that Darken's feet would be everywhere but on the ground and that he would swing around and knock over our display of awards.

Once his feet were in place, someone swung a big bouquet of red plastic flowers in his face, followed by a stick horse which made galloping sounds being waved over his head. The idea was to catch his attention, get him to prick up his ears, arch his neck, and show an alert expression. If you'd like to make a skittery colt come unglued, I can't think of a faster way than surprising him with plastic flowers and a scary stick horse that made noise.

Amazingly, Darken stood his ground, pricked up his ears, and posed like a champion. I, on the other hand, looked like I am expecting him to leap on top of my head or wipe out the decorations at any moment. We came home with a lovely photo of Darken as a beautifully composed and perfectly posed show horse. In contrast, I look like a frazzled mess and only my eyes reveal that I was thinking to myself, "Quick! Snap the photo before anything happens!"

We came, we saw, and we conquered, in spite of a few little bobbles along the way. What an accomplishment for a scaredy-cat colt. I was pleased; Darken just wanted to go home. We loaded up our gear, said goodbye to all our friends, and headed out. Now that the excitement of the show was behind us, the three day journey home seemed like it went on forever. We had a lot to think over as we covered the miles home. We had set a goal for ourselves of competing at the world show, and we had reached it. A lot of time and effort was spent trying to reach that goal, with the hope of victory always in my mind. But once again, looking back, the ribbon and trophy buckle were just the icing on the cake. It was the journey that was the real reward, and I made sure that I savored each day.

Our trip home was, thankfully, uneventful. We spent the night at several fairgrounds along the way, including one which was hosting a Morgan championship show. I toyed with the idea of sneaking Darken into one of the show stalls for the night when no one was looking, but being the only pinto in a barn full of solid colored Morgans, he would have stuck out like a sore thumb. He seemed quite content to spend another night inside the trailer stuffing himself with hay from his newly filled hay bag. He was becoming a better traveler. After putting Darken to bed for the night, I slipped into the arena to watch the Morgan show. Unfortunately, just as I sat down, I saw the tail of the last horse in the last class leave the ring as the announcer said, "Thanks for coming to the show. Have a safe trip home. Goodnight."

Chapter 11

A STAR IS BORN

ONCE HOME, it was back to our usual practice sessions. Every day I continued to work with Darken, trying to help him learn to stay calm and focused. If something startled him, my hope was that he would learn to stop and think about what was happening, rather than just reacting to it. There were times when he frustrated me, and a couple of times I got mad at him, but most of the time I enjoyed the challenge. If I could just figure him out. If I could just keep chipping away at him, I might learn what made him tick, so I could be more effective in his training. I felt that we were teetering on the edge of a major breakthrough.

One day while leading Darken around the indoor arena, he kept pulling me to one particular back corner. I use that same corner to practice with my trick horses because the sand is deeper and softer. Darken, and his sister Dancin, had their stalls on the opposite side of this same arena. Since he seemed determined to get to that corner, I let him, and something amazing happened. He promptly bowed down on both his knees and then popped back up. That was odd. It wasn't uncommon when any of my horses were loose to use that corner, because of the deeper sand, to lie down and roll to scratch their backs. I assumed that he had started to lie down to roll, but changed his mind when something scared him. He often startled himself out of a good roll when he kicked a hoof full of sand against the wall in the process of beginning to lie down.

Then, he bowed down on his knees again. It looked as if he was bowing on purpose. I didn't quite know what to make of it, because if he was bowing on purpose, there was no real reason why he would do so. I had not trained him how to bow. The only possible reason for his new behavior was that he had taught himself. From the vantage point of his stall, he had apparently been watching and learning as the other horses in training practiced their tricks in that same spot.

To test him, I walked him around a bit, took him back to my training spot, cued him to bow by tapping behind his knee with my cue whip, and he bowed. All horses can bow when playing in the pasture, but to do it on cue is a completely different matter. And, it wasn't only the bow that he had taught himself, but to also lay down. He'd lie down and look at me as if to say, "Look what I just did!" That certainly explained what he was trying to do in the middle of the world championship show line up.

From that moment on, Darken became a trick horse whiz kid. He had finally decided it was something he enjoyed and he was very good at it. Since he had shown me that he was now ready to become a trick horse, I set about teaching him more tricks to add to his repertoire. His high energy and ability to spring into the air at a moment's notice had gone from being a liability into being a wonderful asset. His keen eyes picked up on my subtle body movements and he could be controlled with the slightest hand movements. My quick movements were now not something for him to fear, but something I did to communicate with him. Just a wave of my hand could send him off at a canter or stop and turn him in his tracks. Where before he had struggled to understand what I was asking him to do, he now was quickly learning new tricks in a matter of minutes. Now, it was me struggling to keep up with him! With knowledge came confidence and an increased ability and a reason to focus. He was a colt who had suddenly learned he could be a star!

Darken had already taught himself to bow and lie down and with my additional training, he could also perform the Spanish Walk, cross his legs, shake hands, salute, honk a horn, give hugs, act bashful, do the rumba, sit on a bean bag, and many more. He even quickly learned how to stand on that same wooden box that gave him so much trouble as a foal. I would be working in the barn, with him loose in the arena, and I'd hear him—clop, clop, clop, clop—as he jumped up on the wooden platform all by himself. But, he knocked my socks off the day he sat down, flat on the ground from a standing position, just like his mother used to do.

The following year, Darken's sister, Dancin, who is stalled next to him, would do nearly the same thing. I walked into her stall one morning to feed her and she promptly lay down. It seemed rather unusual that she'd put herself in such a vulnerable position. I got her up and down she went again. I thought maybe she was sick. I took her out of her stall and walked her around a bit to see if she was beginning to colic. Just for the heck of it, because of my experience with her brother, I cued her to lie down with a tap of my cue whip behind her hock, and down she went. As with the bow, all horses can lie down, but to lie down on cue is just not something horses do without training, yet I now had two horses that did just that. Apparently, they had been talking to each other and Darken had shared his newfound knowledge.

Chapter 12

SHALL WE TRY AGAIN

DARKEN WAS still a scaredy-cat, but the trick training had given him a whole new direction in life. It gave him a lot more confidence and proved to me just how intelligent he really was. The time seemed right to try riding him again. Colts that get frightened under saddle, or those who buck, are normally not properly prepared. I thought I had adequately prepared him before, but this time, Darken had no excuse. The first time I sat on him, I might have rushed the idea a bit. But by this time, I had spent much more time with him than with any other colt I ever trained. I had done my homework with him and spent hundreds of extra hours working with him in a slow and progressive way. I was pretty confident that things would go better this time; always the optimist.

After my first attempt proved to be a disaster, I was more than a little afraid to try mounting him again. I had a barn full of quiet and gentle horses that I could ride any time I wanted, yet I couldn't wait to try to get back on that slick little black fox. I couldn't wait to find out how he felt to ride. Would he be soft and comfortable or hard and jarring? All horses have a "feel" to them that you can only discover by sitting on their backs. It has a lot to do with their bone structure, muscling, and the angle of their shoulders and pasterns. Some horses look good but ride like a pogo stick, and there is nothing you can do to change it. Others look as if someone sewed two different horses together and yet they ride like you are sitting in an easy chair. You just never know how they will feel, until you actually ride them. Darken was so loose and flexible, he had to feel wonderful. At least I hoped so.

Darken had recently proven that he had remarkable intelligence.

In fact, I was a little worried that he was too smart. It only made sense. His eyes and ears certainly seemed to be highly tuned to the slightest movement and sound. Along with quick eyes and ears, his brain and feet were just as quick. Maybe he was too smart to ever let me ride him.

I was getting older and the idea of being a lawn dart was losing its appeal. It would have been easier to send Darken to a trainer. In fact, if somebody doesn't have the skill and ability to train their own horse, I am the first to recommend they get professional help. I had more than forty years of experience training all types of horses, but I'd never run across a horse quite like Darken. I hadn't counted on him staying so difficult for so long. I'd certainly picked the wrong horse to enjoy the training process, yet I did. It was odd. In the past, I have sold many a horse who "just wasn't working out" or who had this or that perceived flaw. However, with Darken, I had no desire to sell or give up on him, but only an intense desire to figure him out. He wasn't going to get the best of me.

After all the time and effort I had put into Darken's training, I certainly didn't want that hard work undone by anyone who might not have understood him. Timid and sensitive horses tend to over-react to punishment and become even more tense and nervous. I did not want to take the chance that someone might lose their temper with Darken and force him to conform by rough handling.

But, he was not going to be babied either. Just because something scared him was no excuse to climb on top of anyone's head. Nothing is worse than a horse that has become disrespectful of people and is allowed to walk all over them. Darken never showed one ounce of meanness or disrespect, but when one of his senses became overwhelmed, a strong sense of self preservation kicked in. Darken listened very carefully to what Mother Nature had instilled in him and his kind to keep them safe, and it served him well. It was only when I wanted him to be something else that the problems started.

Since my goal with Darken was to enjoy the process, I would stick to my original plan and keep working with him myself. I knew if I could just harness that beauty and intelligence and get him trained to ride, I'd have one special horse. I'd trained dozens of colts, some easy ones and some more difficult, but none had as much natural talent as Darken. Although he often frustrated me, I was lucky to have him.

My problems with Darken weren't from any lack of ability on my part. In fact, I'd trained so many colts that I sometimes got lax and cut a few corners, which often proved to be my downfall with Darken. I normally have a lot of good "horse sense" gained from many years of experience, but once again, I got one of my dumb ideas. I thought since he was doing so well in his ground work, it would be a good idea if I were to hop on him bareback and ride him around in the arena just a little. Not only bareback, but since it was winter time, I was wearing a slippery, crinkly-sounding, nylon snowmobile suit. I knew better, but I did it anyways.

I hopped up on his back, this time without the bucket, grabbed a handful of his mane and encouraged him to take a few steps. He took two steps and started to panic at my presence on his back. His head shot up and he bolted, which quickly turned into bucks. With each big, long, low buck, I had enough time to think about jumping off. Time was running in slow motion.

Just as I would prepare to leap off, he'd stop. I'd decide to stay on, and he'd buck again. He continued bucking the entire length of the arena, and then he stopped. Just when I thought he was done he turned around and bucked back the entire length of the arena. When I finally, shakily, got off, I had a big fistful of his long, black, uprooted mane hair in my hand. Apparently, I was hanging on really well.

Chapter 13

THE OPERATION

UNTIL NOW Darken had been a stallion. Since I didn't need another stallion, I decided to have him gelded. In addition, it was my hope that it would help to settle him down and, as everyone knows, a good stallion makes a great gelding. He had never shown any tendencies toward the aggression that is common with many stallions, so that wasn't a problem. However, my fear was that he might someday get away from me at a show. It would be easy for him to spook at something and pull the lead out of my hand. Since one can never have a loose stallion in public, it would be better for all concerned if he took a new direction in his life and became a gelding.

Still, he was a beautiful horse. People were already asking about breeding their mares to him. No, it was better that he become a gelding and leave the stallion duties to those with calmer temperaments. But still, I would have liked just one foal sired by him before the factory closed. So, I bred him to one of my mares. If the foal had less than perfect conformation, it would still make a nice trail horse. If the foal was perfect, I would kick myself for having Darken gelded. I wanted to do what was best for Darken. As a gelding, he would be able to return to the big pasture where he could join his old playmates from his foal-hood again. I called the vet.

In his usual way, Darken had other ideas. The surgery is normally pretty simple; an operation that is commonly done on the farm. Thousands of colts are gelded each spring. They are given a sedation shot that causes them to peacefully sleep through the whole operation. Being young, they recover quickly and are back eating hay in their stall in short order. The vet clinic sent out one of their young female veterinarians. Although recently out of school, she had several years on staff and was very capable of doing the job at hand.

Darken did not do well with the medication given to sedate him for the surgery. Arabians are tough little buggers and are often equally tough to sedate. Despite being given more medication than a horse his size should have required, he still tried to get up and leave, several times, during his surgery. The poor veterinarian tried valiantly to cover the fact that she was beginning to panic. She was caught between giving him too much sedation, which might kill him, and not giving him enough. Despite a combination of drugs that should have knocked out a Clydesdale, he threw us around like rag dolls. I give the gal credit; she hung in there with him and kept going. It's not a job that you can stop in the middle of very easily.

After his surgery, I was left with instructions to hand-walk him starting the following day, and to keep walking him every day to keep the swelling down and to keep his surgery site open and draining. The next morning I haltered him, got him out, and started walking him around inside the indoor arena. We did a lot of walking and then I got another bright idea. Maybe in his slow and sore state, I might be able to ride him a few laps and save me some boring hand walking. With him wearing only a halter and lead rope, I hopped up onto him bareback and this time he walked around the arena like an old cow, head down and walking slow. This was too easy, but I was surprised to learn that I missed his spark and bounce. I realized something was wrong and quickly slid off him.

I quickly found out why he was so quiet; he was getting sick. He was not his usual springy self and stood very quiet in his stall. When I could reach through his stall bars and touch him unexpectedly without causing him to give a startled jump, I knew something was seriously wrong. The struggling he did during his surgery most likely caused dirt to be kicked up into his surgery site. In spite of all my best follow-up care, he was most likely coming down with an infection. I took him to the vet clinic to be examined. He walked into the clinic with his head down and tail between his legs like a dog that had been kicked. He stood quietly amid doctors, machines, rolling carts, and noisy overhead doors. He never even glanced at the other horses in nearby stalls.

I was right; he was sick and he did have an infection. He was treated, given medication, and sent home. However, he only got sicker. Back to the clinic we went. Again they treated him and sent him back home with instructions for me to keep walking him, hose the surgery site with cold water, and keep him on the antibiotics longer. A few days later, it was very clear he felt worse, much worse. So back to the clinic we went a third time. This time, all the veterinarians at the clinic got together to discuss his case. They said they would have to do surgery again to try to fix the problem once and for all. The original young vet told the head veterinarian that Darken was "difficult" to sedate. With an air of older and more experienced authority, the head vet named off the drugs he would give him. She said that is what she had used. Okay then, he'd add another drug and she told him that she'd used that, too. His confident face changed. "Oh my, he was a difficult one wasn't he?" Because Darken didn't respond well to the original medications he was given, he had to be completely knocked out for this second surgery. Darken was too sick to care what anyone did to him.

I had to leave him overnight. It was a very sad thing to, once again, come home from the vet clinic with an empty trailer. The sick feeling in the pit of my stomach told me that I was very worried that he may never be coming home again. I had two long hard years into him. We had our ups and our downs, but not bringing him back home was unthinkable, but very possible.

The following day, he was sedated, intubated, hooked up to the gas machine, and taken into surgery. He had a pocket of infection the size of a golf ball that the vet said would have never gotten better without the surgery. Once this infection was removed and he finished his medications, he was on the mend and quickly recovered. Always the Drama Queen, Darken had given me another good scare and another big vet bill.

Darken's one and only daughter was born the following year. She was a stunning black and white pinto who grew up to be a wonderful mare. When she was old enough, she too walked the gulf's trails for the first time alongside Tysn, just as her sire had done. Because of her exceptionally quiet behavior, she only required one ponied trip there before she was able to be ridden on the trails solo. She foaled her own solid black filly four years later, making Darken a proud grandfather.

Chapter 14

MORE THAN A ONE TRICK PONY

A SHORT time later, Darken was back to his old self. When he was a stallion he had to be pastured alone so he wouldn't chase the mares. Now that he was a new gelding, he could be turned back into the big pasture, where he had not been since he was a baby.

Tysn stood braced, ready and waiting for him. I expected Tysn was finally going to be able to put this annoying colt in his place. After all, Darken had spent most of his life pestering Tysn over his stall door. Tysn had put up with a lot of this coltish behavior, but his stall door had always protected Darken from Tysn's full strength of teeth and hooves.

Once they were finally together outside, I worried that Tysn might try to kick the poor unsuspecting colt's head right off. Darken just wanted to play, but Tysn might be more interested in proving his dominance. I held my breath as the two stiffly approached each other on tip toes, making a big show of who was the toughest looking. They cautiously stepped within reach of each other, touched noses, and launched into their old game of nippy face nose tag. While there was the occasional disagreement between the two, there would be no serious arguments. Whenever Tysn did try to take a kick at Darken to chase him away from his hay, it was only half-hearted. I needn't have worried about Darken. He was so quick, he was able to dodge teeth and hooves, and still be able to grab a bite of Tysn's hay on the way by.

Darken would spring out of harm's way, then spring in behind him and give Tysn a nip on the tail and spring away again before Tysn knew what hit him. Darken could run circles around him. In the pasture, Darken's ability to spring in any direction at a moment's notice served him well. That same ability nearly unseated me a number of times at the beginning of his saddle training. All it took to send him springing off was the sound of a bit of snow falling from the roof or a hoof full of sand being kicked up against the arena wall. Darken had more spring than a box full of jack rabbits.

Many youth groups and 4-H clubs come to my barn each year to see my trick horses perform and learn how they were trained. The tricks keep the kids' attention while I teach them about being kind to animals, how to take care of their horses and other pets, and to have patience when training them.

Because I knew that the kids' youthful boisterous exuberance would be too much for Darken's sensitive eyes and ears, I always left him in the pasture during these demonstrations. There, he could observe noisy and running children from a safe distance. He always wanted to see and be in on everything happening on the farm, but from a safe distance and where he had room to run away if it became too much for him.

For one particularly large clinic, I forgot and left Darken in his stall until it was too late. The kids were already piling into the barn and getting their seats. Darken needed to overcome his fear of crowds sometime and this time seemed like as good a time as any for him to see kids up close and personal. I would try to keep them away from him as much as possible and just let him look and observe them from the relative safety of his stall.

Once the demonstration got started, I forgot all about Darken. While busy showing the kids another horse's tricks, I looked up and saw a group of kids standing by Darken's stall door. Darken, the horse who thought the world was ending if one of the miniature horses sneezed or the barn cat suddenly appeared, stood pressed against his stall bars so they could reach him more easily. The kids were petting his face, fiddling with his ears, and running their fingers through his mane. There Darken stood, head down, eyes closed, enjoying every minute of it. He earned the right to stay in his stall for all my clinics that day, and he continued to enjoy all our visitors from then on. The kids all wanted him, thinking that he was so gentle and quiet. Beware the wolf in sheep's clothing!

One day a big group of 4-H members came to see the horses. As usual, I used the most advanced trick horses that could always be relied upon to give a perfect performance. Since the kids were eager to see more, I asked if they wanted to see a new trick horse. Of course they did. I prepared them by saying that it was Darken's first time to give a performance for a group. He was very skittish and would probably make mistakes and not be very good, but he would come out and try for them.

With sixty kids sitting on bales of hay in a circle, I brought him out. As I told his story, they were on the edge of their seats. I told the children he wasn't the perfect champion I had expected, he hadn't been easy to train, and nearly everything in his life so far had been a struggle, yet he was a happy horse who tried to do this best. He had had illnesses, accidents, good days and bad. Still, I loved him and had not given up on him. The horse I thought would never amount to much, because he was so timid and over-reactive, had even taught himself tricks. He had already accomplished some amazing things in his young life, and his future looked bright.

It was during this demo that I realized what a wonderful teaching tool he and his story could be. It was okay for him to make mistakes. I could use his mistakes to teach kids to not give up and to keep trying. If he got frightened, I could tell them that everyone gets scared now and then, but they can learn to face their fears just like Darken was doing.

Suddenly, all his silly behaviors became something that could be used to help others. It would be his many challenges that could help kids the most, not his trophies and awards. His story could help kids relate to the troubling things that might be happening in their own lives. Everyone has some roadblocks in their lives, even silly little horses.

When I heard myself tell his story to others for the first time, I was rather stunned to realize that he really was quite an amazing horse. He wasn't a square peg to be hammered into a round hole. He was a goofy and happy colt who was high on life, smart as a whip, and who had his own way of doing things. My job was to go along for the ride and discover and use his talents to the most benefit.

After that, he gave many performances for kids at our barn, where he was most comfortable. I had yet to take him anywhere else to tell his story and to demonstrate his new-found talent, but that was about to change.

Chapter 15

FIRST REAL PERFORMANCE

DARKEN WAS now three and a half years old and at the age I usually start to seriously train my young horses to be ridden. After our earlier stall and bucket disaster and his bucking spree across the arena, I was not looking forward to it. Actually, I was afraid to get back on him. He was quick and as flexible as a cat and probably just as difficult to ride.

Getting on him was always a problem. As far as horses go, at 15 hands tall, Darken is considered on the small side, but still too tall for short little me to climb on easily. I was not about to ever attempt using a bucket again, so I bought an actual mounting block. Forty years of horse training and I'd never owned a real mounting block before. Cowgirls don't need help getting on their horses. However, now that I was getting older and my knees were not what they once were, it seemed like a really good idea. It was a big, green plastic, three-step block that allowed me to easily step into the stirrup. Why had I fought the idea of using a mounting block for so long? It was wonderful. There was still a problem, though. In order for me to mount, Darken had to stand close to the block, which caused me to worry that he'd catch it with a leg or hoof, and again scare himself into a panic, as he had with the bucket.

I girded my loins with all my safety gear, climbed the three stairs of the mounting block, and stepped up on him. He rode off as quietly as a lamb. I was braced for the worst, but it never happened. Darken was forever a puzzlement. Apparently those few laps I had ridden him around the arena, when he was sick, were enough to show him that having me on his back wasn't such a bad thing. When I finally mustered the courage to get back on him, to seriously begin his under-saddle training, I found that he was pretty much already broke. I kept getting little glimpses of just how intelligent he actually was and it caught me off guard every time.

I needn't have worried about him kicking the mounting block and scaring himself. To this day, whenever I climb the mounting block, he comes and positions himself beside the block so I can get on; another self-taught behavior.

Walking and trotting seemed to come easy for him, but I was worried about the canter. I was afraid that adding a little more speed might set off a repeat rodeo. I was getting too old to do a face plant off him. As I rode along at a walk, wondering how I was ever going to dare to ask him to canter, he lifted off into a lovely, slow canter. I had not even asked him. I was just thinking about it, but apparently, that was enough and he had seemingly read my mind. From that day forward, he cantered whenever asked, on the correct lead, without ever being taught. I also never taught him to neck rein, yet he did it effortlessly from that same day. He was a mystery horse for sure.

And that "feel" I wanted to know about? It turned out to be just lovely. He was soft, light, and I felt like I was sitting on a cloud. Only once before had I sat on a horse with such a feel. The feeling was like putting on your favorite sweater and comfortable shoes; like coming home after a long trip.

One day, I got a call from a horse club which asked if I could bring a trick horse to their charity horse show. I had always used my stallion, Black Tie, for demos and clinics away from home. Black Tie earned his oats by not only performing flawlessly, but by always being able to be counted on to stand like a statue among kids and wheel chairs in noisy and crowded places. He even once performed at a state fair with a helicopter ride taking off and landing all day right next to him. Black Tie was nearing retirement, so it was time for me to be training his replacement. Darken had never done a trick demonstration anywhere but at home, but it was time for him to give it a try.

I took the chance and hauled Darken five hours to the event. We arrived the evening before the show and he came out of the trailer tense and spooking at everything in sight. I began to worry that I had brought the wrong horse. I was now too far away from home to go back and get Black Tie. I would have to make do with the horse I brought. I looked through the barn to find a stall which had a solid door, so if Darken panicked, he could not jump out. I worried all night that he would be so distracted by all the new sights and sounds, that he would be unable to perform his tricks.

Since I was there, I took Darken in a few halter classes the following morning. This gave him a chance to get into the ring before his performance, and he behaved fairly well. Intermission came all too quickly and soon it was time for Darken's first performance of the day. To add to our pressure, the host club had bussed in residents of a local group home, so they could watch the horse show. They all had been told that there would be a special trick horse performance, and they excitedly took their seats, ready to be entertained. I was afraid that there would be no show and that Darken would merely prance around, ignoring my cues.

I took a deep breath and lead Darken into the large outdoor ring at a trot. I started off by asking him to perform a few simple tricks, which he did quite handily. Surprisingly, he went through all of his tricks flawlessly. He watched my body language and obeyed all my cues and performed like he'd been an exhibition trick horse all his life.

I could not believe how well he did for his first big solo performance. He put all his bounce and spring to good use and performed trick after trick with joy. As a trick horse, he was no longer a scaredy-cat, but a performer. He even perfectly performed his most difficult trick, the sit, in front of the packed stands, just like his mother used to do. He was a real hit with the crowd, especially the children.

Back at the barn, I put him in his stall to wait for his second performance of the day. I checked back in on him a little later and found something weird in his stall. It was about the size and shape of a lamb, all rolled up, and covered in sawdust. What the heck was that? Darken had reached under his door, grabbed his neighbor's saddle blanket, pulled it into his stall, and had a wonderful time rolling it around in his sawdust bedding. Sheepishly, I retrieved the blanket, brushed off the sawdust, and returned it to its rightful owner. Not only could he entertain others, he could also entertain himself. This goofy little horse was really endearing himself to me.

Chapter 16

HITTING THE TRAILS

BACK HOME Darken was riding pretty well inside the indoor riding arena, but I had not dared ride him one step outside the arena. He was, as yet, just too spooky and flighty to try. He'd snort and spook at simply the excitement of being some place different, even if it was just on the other side of his pasture fence.

Even when something would surprise him in his own pasture, he'd bolt away with his tail flung over his back, looking over his shoulder at the imagined threat. Seeing nothing, he'd bolt away again. A plastic water tub that wasn't where it was supposed to be was cause for great concern. He'd take a closer look and seeing no danger, would bolt away and return a moment later for another look. What a nut! I swear he looked for things to give him an excuse to act silly, as he wasn't really afraid of it anymore.

The time came to try his first trail ride. While working alone is definitely not the smartest way to start a young horse, if I want to do anything, alone is how I must do it. For me, there are fewer distractions if I can work with a young horse one-on-one.

To be safer, my plan was to first pony Darken down some easy trails with his old pal, Tysn. I would ride Tysn and lead Darken beside him. I hauled them both the short distance to a neighborhood park where there were easy and open bridle trails.

We live in a small rural town with the funny name of Ashtabula, which is located in the upper northeastern corner of Ohio. The Ashtabula River runs through the middle of it, so named and pronounced by the Algonquin Indians as "Hash-tah-bul-lah", which means "River of Many Fish".

The trails that run along this river are within a park system called the Indian Trails, which opened in 1908 and encompasses 405 acres, so named for the riverside paths used by the Indians who once hunted in that area. Their paths wound along the Ashtabula River where it passed through a deep and beautiful gorge, as deep as 70 to 125 feet in places and six or seven miles long, set against a backdrop of spectacular shale cliffs. Officially, the gorge is called the Ashtabula River Gulf, but locals simply call this area "the gulf".

The gulf gained worldwide attention on December 29, 1876 when it became the unenviable location of the Ashtabula Railroad Bridge Disaster. The 150 foot metal railroad bridge spanning the gulf fell 70 feet into the river, causing great loss of life. Among those lost in the disaster, were famous hymn writer P.P. Bliss and his wife, Lucy. In 2008, another bridge was built over the gulf at the opposite end of the park. This 613 foot bridge, called the Smolen-Gulf Bridge, is the longest covered bridge in the United States, and the fourth longest in the world. Ashtabula County is home to 17 covered bridges.

During the summer months, the river is barely ankle deep, but come early spring or late fall it swells to monstrous proportions, making crossing it impossible. The river ends a few miles away, where it flows into Lake Erie. Because of the depth and size of the gulf, when you are down in the bottom, it feels like you are miles from anywhere, yet parts of it are within sight of downtown Main Street. There are beautiful high shale banks on both sides, lots of trees, and river crossings. There are usually a few fishermen there year round—someone who could call for help should I need it. It is a good place near home to take a colt on his first trail ride. There was another plus, which I pushed to the back of my mind; where I planned to ride was less than ten minutes from the local rescue unit and hospital.

Twelve years earlier, I had first taught Tysn himself to be ridden on the same trails. On his first solo ride he startled a few times at the odd, scary-looking fallen log, and then quickly settled into being a calm, steady, trusted trail horse. After that, and with lots of additional training, he went on to win many show championships. Tyson was that easy, no muss no fuss.

Since then, Tysn ponied many a youngster on its first outing. By staying calm, Tysn would show them how trail riding was done and that there was nothing to fear. The colts were always excited at first, but quickly settled in and enjoyed getting out and doing something new. A number of the training colts were so quiet, they didn't need the security of another horse and were able to hit the trails solo their first time out. Darken was definitely not one of these colts.

Once at the park, I unloaded the horses, saddled Tysn, and clipped a long lead rope to Darken's halter. As I rode Tysn and led Darken from the parking lot, across the road and into the trails, we came to a row of huge stone blocks. They are placed there to keep ATVs off the trails, leaving just enough room for hikers and horseback riders to fit between them. Darken had not yet figured out how this ponying idea went, and was bouncing all over the place. I rode Tysn between the blocks, expecting Darken to follow along behind us. He didn't. He squatted down and leaped over the huge wall of blocks like a deer, scaring the wits out of me. Poor Tysn, he must have wondered what was wrong with this young colt he was expected to mentor. He was not amused, but he tolerated the greenhorn as Darken constantly bumped into him in an effort to avoid a tree branch here or mud puddle there.

After the surprise with the stone blocks and Tysn's calm example,

Darken actually seemed to enjoy getting out on the trails. He'd walk along beside Tysn, looking left and right, and then prick his ears toward some noise he heard off in the distance. When we came to the river crossing, I expected him to refuse to get his feet the least tiny bit wet. Instead, he waded right in up to his knees, as if he'd done it all his life. He was a constant puzzle. Just when I was thinking that I might be able to switch horses, Darken would hear or see something that startled him and he'd leap ahead, trying to bolt away. Nope, not ready to switch horses yet.

After more practice at home and another ponied ride with Tysn, it was time to try riding Darken alone on the trails. The idea of switching back and forth between pony horse and Darken seemed like an accident waiting to happen...too many reins and ropes to get tangled up in if the unexpected happened. I decided to go it alone.

I hauled Darken back down to the gulf. After a bit of longeing in the parking lot, to wear him down a little, I got ready to take the plunge. I put my business card in my pocket; this would provide vital information if rescue workers needed it after finding my unresponsive body along the trail. I had carefully tried to prepare Darken the best I could and I didn't really think I would have any real problems. If I'd really thought he was unsafe to ride there alone, I would not have attempted it. I expected him to act like most colts do when going solo for the first time—nervous and jumpy. I was prepared for that. It's interesting that horse people think about what could happen, prepare for such events, and then get on a horse anyway. Optimists, all of us!

I strapped on my helmet, put my cell phone in my pocket, buck-led my protective vest, hopped on his back, got a good grip on my grab strap, and we headed down the easier trail on the north side of the valley. It was shorter, flatter, and with fewer obstacles than the longer and more difficult trails across the street to the south. Darken was very hesitant and cautious, looking left and right and practically walking on his tip toes, but he walked along much better than I had expected. When he heard the noise of the waterfall ahead, he stopped and listened, but with encouragement walked on past it. What a good boy! It was short, it was sweet, and before something bad happened, we ended his first trail ride on a good note and went home. And besides, I couldn't have held my breath much longer.

On his second ride, I had planned to again ride on the easy trails, but someone running a chainsaw nearby made me reconsider. Riding next to a chainsaw on a horse on his second solo trail ride did not seem like a good idea. Instead, we would ride across the street where the more difficult trails and eight water crossings were. The first obstacles we encountered were the same huge stone blocks that Darken had jumped while being ponied from Tysn. He took one look at those blocks and froze. I had no intention of giving him the opportunity to leap them with me on his back, so I dismounted and carefully lead him through. He eyed them on both sides and skittered quickly through, tail tucked tight between his hind legs.

The woods were beautiful. It was fall and while the leaves on the trees were still mostly yellow, they were beginning to float down. I had forgotten that one important fact. The falling leaves made a thick blanket on the ground, a blanket of crunchy, noisy leaves that magnified the sound of any movement in the woods and covered over any muddy spots, branches, or rocks. Darken was terrified, and I was so nervous I was sweating.

We could hear what sounded like someone or something walking toward us through the dry leaves. Riding alone can be scary enough, but riding alone on a skittish young horse amid the sounds of strangers we couldn't see is even scarier. Not only do other horses use these same trails, but many fisherman, hikers, and dog walkers. At any moment, one of them could make an unexpected appearance from around the next bend and spook Darken. Worse yet, campers, who are not supposed to be there, occasionally pitch their tents deep in the foliage and suddenly pop out of their tents to see who is near their hiding places. And, there is always the chance of coming across drug deals going down, naked skinny dippers, or just plain weirdoes. Darken walked along wanting to run, but not knowing which direction to go first. His muscles were tense and I was bracing for a possible panicked spin or quick bolt in any direction.

The high gulf walls were on both sides of us as we rode along the beginning of the trail that led into the woods. The high banks cut off two directions of flight, so I began to feel trapped as we walked deeper into the darkening trails. Knowing that there could be any number of unsavory individuals hidden amidst the underbrush only heightened the tension. The sounds were all around and worse... above us. It turned out to be dozens of squirrels running through the dried leaves. On the steep banks, on either side of us, scampered huge gray squirrels as large as small cats. Apparently the living was good in the gulf, and they were running here and there trying to hide their bounty of nuts for the winter.

As we walked deeper into the woods, Darken caught sight of the squirrels and quickly figured out they were the cause of the sounds.

The Indians could have easily named the place "Banks of Many Squirrels". I was fooled at first, too. I thought the sounds were either people or deer walking near us. At any moment they might pop out and scare us, causing Darken to wheel and bolt, and me to wish I'd brought a change of underwear. We both gave a huge sigh of relief.

As we continued our ride, my little equine friend experienced mud, fallen logs, hills, more squirrels, ravines, and the river, for the first time alone, and did surprisingly well. There might be hope for him under saddle yet.

I had brought a long rope with me, in case I had to dismount and lead Darken through something he might perceive as particularly scary. When we came to a washed out section of trail, rather than take the risk of a flying leap through it, I dismounted and used the long rope to lead him across it. Once back on him, I coiled up the rope and looped it around the saddle horn. A steeper ravine was just ahead and I would probably need it again. No sense in securing it to the saddle I thought, just to take it off again in a minute.

As we began down into the narrow ravine, which leads straight down and directly into the river, I noticed something was dragging behind us, causing Darken to tuck his tail and scoot ahead. Looking back over my shoulder, it appeared that something was caught in his tail. It looked like a thin tree branch, but turned out to be my uncoiled rope dragging from the saddle horn and tugging on his tail. I needed to quickly dismount and remove it before he panicked. As I went to dismount, I got my right pant leg caught on the loose cantle plate on the back of my saddle. It was then that I noticed that a long stick had run up between his bridle cheek piece and his face near his eye.

There we stood, teetering on the side of a muddy ravine headed straight down into the river, a stick stuck in his bridle at one end, a rope caught in his tail on the other end, and me with my pants caught on the back of the saddle. Poor Darken was tangled up at both ends with me stuck in the middle. I got myself unstuck and then got everything else straightened out on Darken. We continued on our way with no more excitement. On the way back home, he crossed the bad sections of the trail on his own without being led across. Another accomplishment! He probably had his mind set on just getting back to the safety of the trailer and going home, and wasn't going to let muddy ravines or silly squirrels stop him.

Chapter 17

THE FISH

THE DAY came when three of my lady friends asked me to go on a trail ride with them. Since the ride was in the same gulf that Darken had been ridden in before, I figured there was no time like the present to try riding him in company. At home I ride alone, so Darken never had the opportunity to ride with others, or to be asked to go to the right, while everyone else went to the left.

As I unloaded him in the parking lot, he was all snort and blow. He threw his tail over his back and flew around on the longe line as I attempted to wear him out a little. He looked left and right over his shoulder at the other horses and kept craning his neck to see what they were doing while their owners saddled them up. As one of the gals stepped out of her trailer's dressing room and slammed the door, Darken threw his head up at the sound, tucked his tail, and bolted to the other end of the parking lot with me in tow. Oh boy, this ride was not going to be fun.

Of the three mares going on the ride, Sable was the most seasoned trail horse. She was a chestnut Spotted Saddle Horse that never put a hoof wrong, the picture of a reliable trail mount. The other two horses were Moriah, a beautiful palomino Quarter Horse, and Storm, a magnificent huge black draft cross. They had been to the gulf many times before and it was old hat to them. Darken was the odd man out, the only male in the group, and the only true greenie.

I tacked up Darken and climbed aboard. He felt like riding a rubber band, craning his head around to keep an eye on each horse. With all the other horses headed out to the trailhead, Darken had his eyes glued to where they were going, and he wasn't about to be left behind. I explained to the gals that this was only my third time riding him on the trail and that any moment I might be lying on the ground wondering what happened. They laughed. To my surprise, Darken walked along behind the group like a trooper. They commented on how well he was doing. Since all of them had trained their own horses, they knew the situation could change in a heartbeat.

The first obstacle we encountered, right past the parking lot, were those dreaded stone blocks. In his rush to stay up with the other horses, Darken skittered warily between them. Occasionally he'd hear or see something that startled him and his head would quickly raise; he'd tuck his tail, prepared to dash off in one direction or another, but he kept walking along, afraid he'd miss something. He crossed the river and climbed over rocks and fallen logs like a horse that had trail ridden for years.

Riding in a group is a good thing, as you always have someone to help you, a built in rescue squad in case of an emergency, or at the very least, someone to call 911 for you. Their quiet horses are good examples for green horses to learn from. The disadvantage of group riding is that the group might decide to do something that you're not prepared to do, and do so without telling you first.

We were riding along at a walk, admiring the pretty trees, the river, and chitchatting about life. The ladies were impressed with how Darken was doing, never guessing that under my smile, I was worried. I knew how quickly he could overreact to anything unexpected.

Although they could not see it, I could feel his muscles tighten and relax as he intermittently prepared to leap left or right at a moment's notice. His head would jerk upright as he stared, transfixed on some object along the trail, then relax until the next scary thing caught his eye. Then it happened. The riders ahead decided that this particular stretch of trail was a good place to gallop, and, without a word of warning, or perhaps being at the end of the line I just didn't hear it, off they went. Darken suddenly noticed that his new little herd had left without him. Since they were running, something dreadful must have happened, and he wanted to run for cover, too.

When I ride, I practice the slow controlled gaits required in the show ring. I strive for a relaxed horse, bending and flexing easily to my aids and cues. When we walk, I want my horse to move in a long-strided, relaxed, and flat-footed walk on a loose rein. When we jog, it's a slow and cadenced movement. I had never allowed Darken to go faster than a slow controlled canter. The thought that we might be doing a wild Indian gallop through the woods this early in his under saddle training hadn't even occurred to me.

When the group raced off ahead of us, all of Darken's training went right out the window. I found myself sitting atop a coiled spring that was fighting to fly after them. I could either be left behind sitting on a horse having a meltdown because of being suddenly abandoned, or go with the flow. Not that I had that much control of the situation, but we went with the flow. I must have had my mouth open, as I suddenly found myself with one of Darken's furry black ears in my mouth, tickling my tonsils. He uncoiled and released his pent-up body energy forward into a full gallop.

I am not afraid of a little speed, but I am afraid of speed combined with uneven ground on a horse who isn't even noticing the hills and dips he's charging over. At any moment Darken could take a tumble, with me on the bad end of a fall. Up ahead, the girls galloped on with unfettered glee, completely unaware of the black rocket closing in on their horses' tails. Trees and twisted fallen logs, which at a walk would have caused Darken great concern, were flying past us without a second glance. His head was held so high; his long black mane was whipping me in the face. Darken's intent was to catch up and stick with his fleeing herd, and he made good on his intent.

As they came to a downgrade at a river crossing, the girls slowed their horses to a sedate walk as they prepared to cross. Every spring and fall, northeastern Ohio is descended upon by fishermen who flock to our Ashtabula River to fish for trout. The anglers were out in full force today.

The fishermen all looked the same, dressed to the ears in fishing gear. Since this was early fall and the river was still low, it seemed ridiculous for them to be wearing waders up to their armpits while fishing in four inches of water. The big fish lay hidden in the scattered deep holes here and there, and this is where all the anglers were poised and waiting. Unfortunately, one of those holes was located just where we had to cross the river. We apologized to the fisherman as we trudged through the water between them, churning up the water and most likely scaring away every fish within ear shot.

Darken's blood, racing after his unexpected dash through the woods at breakneck speed, was still pumped up as we went into the water. He was glued to the back end of Storm, the big black mare in front of us. Like a life line, he wasn't about to let her get out of his sights again. He didn't seem to notice that he was getting splashed in the face each time one of her massive rear hooves plunged into the water. He was completely unaware that, by trying to follow so close-ly, she could have killed him with one kick. He had already suffered one skull fracture as a two year old; he didn't need a second one.

As our group trooped through the water, one of the fish for which the men had probably waited all day, was driven from its hid-ing place by our horses' hooves. It came out of its deep hole and made a break for the next one across the shallow open waters. I saw him as he swam out from behind Storm and watched in horror as he swam between Darken's front legs. I could see its fins sticking out of the water as it franticly flopped and splashed about in the shallow water and rocks under us. The fish was a trout, had lots of fins, and looked to be about seventeen inches long. Who knew such big fish were in such shallow waters? Amid the horses' splashing, the fish made it to the temporary safety of the next hiding hole, much to the displeasure of the fishermen.

Darken was so concerned about being left behind, he never took his eyes off Storm's big, black, wavy tail ahead of him. He missed seeing and feeling the fish entirely. Had he been alone when the huge fish torpedoed toward him and flopped around between his legs, he would have wheeled around and walked on water to beat it back to the safety of the dry banks.

The rest of the ride passed without too much drama. Other than for the brief moment I had one of Darken's ears down my throat, it wasn't too bad for his first group trail ride.

Chapter 18

THE GIFT

MY MAIN trick horse, Black Tie, was getting on in years and I was using Darken more often to replace him. One day I got a call to do a trick performance for a group sponsoring a major trail ride and, once again, Darken was called upon to perform. He and I had spent so much time together that we were now beginning to have an understanding between us. I could read him like a book and could usually stay one step ahead of him. I knew his every move, and he knew mine. During our performances, it was becoming possible to turn him on and off like a light switch. When I needed him to leap into the air, he could do so effortlessly, and when I needed him to stand still, he could do that too. We were finally becoming partners. He listened for his cues better now, instead of worrying so much about what was going on around him. He was a horse who really benefited from the consistent handling, repetition, patience, and positive reinforcement that the trick training gave him.

Because of his work with children, Chimacum Tack Shop of Texas donated, to Darken, a beautiful custom-made white circus-horse harness. It was covered in red and blue jewels that flashed in the sun and his bridle was topped with a feather plume, which I could change to match my different outfits. It was sometimes difficult to know just what ran through Darken's head, but I knew from the first time he wore his new harness, he was a different horse with it on. He was proud, and he knew what it was for. It was just what he needed.

When our turn came to perform, Darken's mind was focused on his job. I was very pleased with him. Several times while I was answering questions from the audience, he was so relaxed and his head was so low, his ears rubbed my knees. People asked questions as to his breed, and remarked how quiet he was. He was so quiet that I worried that they might think he was sedated. It was the first time that he really understood that he had a job to do. He knew the job and he did it. Having ears too low was much better than having them crammed down my throat, as in our first group trail ride.

Back at the trailer, he got his after-performance carrots while people stopped by to ask more questions about him and his training. Outside of the ring, Darken was a bit more nervous and fidgety, but it gave me the opportunity to tell the children about the many challenges in his life and how he was still working at overcoming them. He was still a work in progress, but I was seeing that he really enjoyed his job. We both went home happy campers.

Chapter 19

DRESSAGE PRACTICE

DARKEN AND I had been practicing very hard and he was making great progress. I was itching to get him in the show ring, under saddle, to see how he would do. He was five years old now and I'd been riding him in lessons with my students for several months. Taking him to an under-saddle show was beginning to become a possibility. He was becoming more confident in places he had been to before, but he easily became unnerved in new locations. The sight and sound of running horses was still causing him worry and concern. Again, when Mother Nature whispered in his ear, Darken listened. Trying to show him in a ring with twenty running horses didn't seem like a good idea yet. For his first under-saddle show, I needed to find one which offered classes where he could compete alone in the ring, until he was more experienced. Dressage seemed like just the thing Darken needed.

Dressage tests each horse, one at a time as an individual, and reveals whether or not the training of your horse is on track. The word dressage means training. Not only could Darken be in the ring alone, but the training would, hopefully, be very helpful in the development of both his body and his mind. Dressage emphasizes the development of such desirable qualities as balance, suppleness, submission (lightness to the aids), straightness, freedom of movement, harmony with rider, and most importantly to Darken, obedience and relaxation.

Just as in trick training, dressage training is done in a progressive way. Each stage, or level, is based on the foundation of previous work. Most horses start at the bottom and, as they master each test, they advance up the levels. Horse and rider are expected to perform a series of predetermined movements in a rectangular arena measuring

60 x 20 meters. Twelve lettered markers are placed symmetrically around the rail to indicate where movements are to start and finish, including invisible letters down the center line of the ring. A judge sits at one end of the ring and watches each team, while a scribe writes down her comments. The judge scores each movement with a score from 0 to 10, with most scores somewhere in the middle. Once the scores are totaled, they produce a percentage; the horse and rider with the highest percentage wins.

Darken had already learned many of the skills he would need. He could do them easily at home, but could he be counted on to perform them anywhere else? He had surprised me and become a trick horse when I didn't think it was possible. Could he surprise me again and become a dressage horse? I was about to find out.

I found an upcoming schooling dressage show and entered him. Unrated schooling shows are good places to take a young horse for his first experiences in dressage competition. I had not ridden a dressage test myself in eight years. The search was on for my old dressage clothes. When one is in her fifties, eight years can result in a lot of body changes.

At their price, I was not going to buy new show clothes just for two classes. I would make my old ones fit. Because they were made of industrial strength material, I was still able to pull and tug my way into my old white breeches. Thank goodness their strength and stretch held up. By sitting up tall and straight, I was still able to button my jacket, but if I slouched, I'd pop my buttons. I would have to sit up straight for sure. The shirt, however, sadly gapped by four inches and would have to be replaced. A quick trip to the tack store fixed the too-tight shirt problem. I did wonder, as I was trying it on in front of the tack shop mirror; if I fell off while wearing it, would it ever again be such an eye-popping white.

In preparation for the show, I had Darken shod. Two days later he was lame. I checked him each day and each day was different. First he limped on his left front leg, then his right front leg, then his left back leg, then all three, then one front leg. Of course, I'd already paid my entry fees to the show and now it looked as if I'd wasted my hard earned money. I pulled his shoes off and in a couple of days he was sound again. The show would go on! It would take some additional investigation to discover what was causing him to be lame while wearing shoes. With Darken, it was just one more of his many mysteries.

The show was on a Sunday. For those coming from out of town, the farm, where the show was to be held, offered overnight boarding. If you were local, like I was, and wanted to come in the evening before the show just to school your horse, you could do so for an additional $15.

On Saturday night I took Darken to the show grounds and paid my practice fee. He'd never been to the grounds before. As soon as we arrived, I began to do a quick look around to see where the horse-eating monsters were lurking, so I could be prepared for them and not caught off guard. Darken had become pretty dependable in familiar surroundings, especially when performing his tricks. However, in a new location without the security of a job he knew well, he was tense and nervous. Entering new territory brought up all his old fears again. He stood frozen in his tracks and looked bug-eyed at everything. The trash can, the flag pole, and even the plastic pipe under the driveway all startled him and caused him to shy away from them.

The grounds had three well-manicured outdoor show rings surrounded with lovely, low, white painted fences. At the end of each ring was a small building that looked like a child's play house. This is where the judge and her scribe would be seated, out of the sun and weather, during the show. For some reason, even normally quiet horses find these buildings scary, especially when their doors are open, revealing a dark interior.

While we were not allowed to ride inside the actual show rings, we could ride around the outside of them and let our horses see all the spooky spots. As I walked Darken toward the show rings, he spied the white plastic chains that lined the walkways. He blew air through his nose and pricked his ears at them, then froze. Oh dear, what had I done? Tomorrow's show was going to be a nightmare; he was not ready for this yet. Given the quality of the other horses and the talent of their riders, I should have taken Darken's training a lot more seriously before entering him in even a schooling show. The other horses there for practice were huge in comparison to my little slinky black fox. They were tall, elegant warm bloods, thoroughbreds, and horses that clearly were born to be dressage horses. For their practice sessions their riders rode in sporty schooling attire that came from expensive dressage boutique stores. Their boots and breeches all came with a price tag that would choke…well, a horse. We were clearly out of our element.

Darken barely noticed I was on his back as I did my best to control him. His head was up and he shied away from everything we approached. The black plastic bags inside the trash cans were nearly the end of him. Always on the alert for what would set off a nervous horse, I spotted a mother Killdeer sitting on her nest of three spotted eggs directly beside the dressage letter "E". As we passed by her, she'd stand up, straddle over her eggs, and fluff up her plumage to make herself bigger. Meanwhile, her husband would screech and do his best to make you believe that he had broken his wing, in an effort to lure you away from their nest. When riding the tests the following day, I would have to place my horse's feet within inches of the nest several times during our ride. I could just see Darken stomping on the bird's toes and having her burst out from under him in a screeching, feathered panic. Exit stage left for Darken and a face plant in the dirt, most likely, for me. I warned all the other riders, who hadn't noticed the unhappy bird; they had no need to be looking for monsters behind every stone. It was beneath their well-schooled horses' dignity to have been afraid of all the silly things that would alarm Darken.

Next, he noticed the boys next door, bouncing a basketball off a metal hoop in their yard. Each basket would make a weird double "waaaang" sound, which made Darken's ears search for the source of the sound like two black radar towers. Next, he skittered past the big oil well pump that sat near the corner of Ring 4. Thank goodness it was not running or he might never have gotten near it. However, the worst troll he found was a giant weeping willow tree within a few yards of the show ring rail. Our home trees, and those we'd met on the trails, were tall stately trees. They stood up tall and minded their own business, except when they were shedding their leaves down on us in the fall. This willow tree bent in the wind and reached its whip-like arms out at us as we passed. Darken took one look, tucked his tail tight to his butt cheeks, scooted past, then whipped his head around to stare, "What the heck *was* that thing?"

As the wind blew its branches, they bent low then swung out at us again and Darken ducked his body away from it, while still keeping his eye on it over his shoulder. After a couple of trips back and forth beside it, each time Darken giving it a wide berth, I thought it a good idea to let him get close enough to sniff the branches. Why do I get these ideas and then act on them? I took him up close, let him sniff, and he grabbed a big mouth full of the leaves. Of course, when he pulled back to tear them off, they didn't break, but instead pulled the whole branch toward him, scaring the pants off him. I could easily see "willow tree leaves" written on my chart as the reason I was in the emergency room. As he leaped away, teeth clenched, the mouthful tore off and he was rewarded with twelve inches of green willow branch. In the end, it was Darken 1, willow tree 0.

On Friday night, I lay awake trying to memorize the two tests I had entered. "Down center line turn right, or was it left?" My dyslexic mind was too busy trying to memorize my tests to shut off and sleep. The thoughts kept rolling over and over in my head all night. In order to memorize a dressage test, I have to picture myself riding it, or get off my horse and walk it. If I read the test, or see it on paper, it's meaningless to my brain and doesn't stick in my memory. Not only am I dyslexic, and everything I read is backwards to me, but I am also allergic to all things horse related—sawdust, hay, mold, and the dust in their coats. I have my own set of road blocks. I just deal with them and trudge on.

Chapter 20

FIRST DRESSAGE SHOW

ON SATURDAY night, I slept just fine. Sunday morning came, and off to the show we went. Dressage shows are often populated by several types of riders; kids on ponies just having fun, beginners struggling to enter the world of dressage, the ones who have ridden for years and just can't advance much further than the lower levels for a whole host of reasons, the ones who are seriously working their way up the ladder, and the dressage queens who are all striving to be at the very top of their sport. The queens are those who take dressage very seriously and they can be very intimidating. They have invested a small fortune in lessons and a winning horse that can do the job. As they practice, one is impressed by their riding skills and their horses' training.

Thankfully, they have long ago progressed to the advanced classes and my green horse and I would not have to compete against them. That's the beauty of dressage; you compete against horses at your level. However, even at the lower levels, there are those who clearly are ahead of the game and are very impressive. It's watching them, while you are sitting at the in-gate that makes you seriously reconsider entering the class in the first place. As you watch them ride, it is easy to second-guess your decision to compete.

Soon, it was time to get dressed and warm up Darken. My breeches were a tight fit on a good day, but on a humid day, it was going to take superhuman effort to get them on. I shimmied and slithered and wedged myself into them. Good thing I was alone in the dressing room. After everything was on, I stood looking into the mirror. I was a gleaming spectacle in snow white, until I put on my black coat. What was I thinking? One good bird-bursting spook and someone would be helping me to limp, sad and dirty, to the out-gate while a flock of spectators and grooms went dashing off to catch my fleeing horse.

My ride time of 11:56 was getting closer. What a weird feeling. Everything was set in place to funnel me ever closer to the in-gate. I have shown horses for over forty years, yet there I sat, with butterflies in my stomach, at a schooling show. Perhaps it was because I knew Darken so well; I could usually read his thoughts and knew his fears, and I worried that I was asking too much of him.

I tacked up my horse, got on, and rode him toward the warm up ring. The wheels were set in motion and I couldn't stop it. I was going to have to go through with it. My test pattern rolled around and around inside my head. "Down center line, halt at X, salute the judge, wait for her return salute, turn left, then what?"

As Darken entered the warm-up ring, where the night before he'd eyed the bushes along the rail with great suspicion, he heaved a huge sigh. As we walked along, he sighed again. I was immediately more at ease. The $15 practice night was worth every penny!

As we got closer to the ring, I learned that the bird and her eggs had been relocated that morning. I didn't have to worry about that anymore. The wind was no longer making the willow whip its branches about. Another thing I don't have to worry about. I was beginning to heave my own sighs of relief.

My entry number was a small, round cardboard thing that clipped to the side of Darken's bridle, between his eye and ear. At each step, it moved and its metal clip tapped on the metal of his bridle buckles.

People have been bucked off a spooky horse over less. I lowered the buckle so it no longer tapped on the entry number backing and we were good to go. Problem solved and Darken didn't even seem to notice that it was dangerously close to attacking his ear or poking him in the eye.

As I sat on him, looking at the number clipped to his bridle, I noticed how loose the bridle brow band was. My other horse, Black Tie, really filled out a bridle. Like a typical Arabian horse, Black Tie's head was short and compact, but wide across the forehead. We used to joke that it was because Arabians have such massive brains that they need larger brow bands. Darken wore the same bridle, like a kid wears his father's shoes. I was suddenly very aware that he was just a youngster, his clothes not quite fitting his growing frame. All this was so new to him. It made me even more aware that I was not sitting on my faithful, confident, friend of twenty years, but on a new dancing partner.

With two riders ahead of me, I was funneled into a waiting area, just steps away from the ring; the same ring we had not been allowed to set hoof in during practice. I felt like I was sitting in a plane, slowly taxiing down the runway, waiting to be next to take off. The take-off part was what I was worried about. As I watched the rider two ahead of me, while trying to sear the test pattern into my brain, her horse bolted and she was bucked off. There she lay, her pretty white clothes in contact with last night's rain soaked black arena footing. She lay exactly at the spot I had envisioned would be my trouble spot, just past the judge's stand. Off went her bay horse, running across two rings while everyone was screaming, "Loose horse!" For a moment, even though I held Darken's reins in my hand, I actually looked to see if he was still there, and not the loose horse that everyone was yelling about and running after.

On Saturday, we had practiced going past that small judge's stand. Two girls sat inside each stand; and most riders had practiced going past the building, giving their horses lots of time to notice the people inside. I took a handful of treats out of my pocket and had the girls feed them to Darken as we walked up to the stand. I was glad that I had practiced riding past them with moving people inside.

The loose horse was caught, the fallen exhibitor helped off to sit in the air-conditioned first aid room for the rest of the afternoon, and the horse ahead of me was beginning to exit the ring. We were next. We made one warm-up lap around the outside of the ring, past the judge's stand where two new people sat, ready to judge us. I let Darken take a good look at the suspicious looking characters sitting inside. Would they know this was his first time inside a ring under saddle and be forgiving, or would they be horrified that my horse performed like a drunken sailor and score us accordingly? I almost mentioned it to them, then thought better of it, and would take my chances.

Darken performed as if he'd shown dressage his entire life. After his tense practice night, his good behavior caught me completely off guard. He concentrated on the task at hand, listened to my cues, and never put a hoof wrong. I was prepared to come crawling out of the ring after providing jolly entertainment for the spectators, and was instead congratulated for a job well done. People were asking who that little black horse was, that no one had seen there before. What breed was he? Who *was* he?

An hour later, we were back in the ring for our second test and we had a repeat performance. He was nearly flawless. He ended the day earning his first two blue ribbons under saddle, with scores ten points higher than his closest competitor. I was overjoyed, but puzzled. Now I had no explanation why he was so good.

As I led him to the trailer to go home, I noticed one of the dressage queens, who had had a young horse in both my classes, walking her horse toward her trailer ahead of us. Although still fairly young, her horse was big, pretty, impressive, and most likely very expensive. As she got to her trailer, she threw her horse's lead rope up and over his back, expecting him to obediently walk into the trailer on his own. He didn't. She circled him around and repeated the same command. Again, her horse refused. By now, I was to the back of my own trailer with Darken. I opened the door and glanced over at her parked next to us. Since she was having trouble, I didn't want her to catch me staring. She was now tapping her horse's hindquarters with her whip and her horse was sashaying side to side, getting more upset by the moment. Darken stepped up to the back edge of our trailer and stopped. I sneaked another peek over at the queen. Her horse was now leaping side to side while she was whacking at it harder with her whip. I looked back at Darken and whispered to him, "If you are ever going to get into this trailer quickly, do it now. I know they are watching." He raised his head, hesitated for a split second, then stepped up into the trailer. As we pulled out of the parking lot, I glanced back to see her, now with help, still trying to get her fancy horse in her trailer. Darken 2. Dressage Queen 0.

Back at home, Darken celebrated with an apple and a big dinner, and then probably spent the rest of the night repeating his day's victory to his stable mates, until they couldn't stand to hear the story again. I headed to the shower, and then talked my husband into going out for a victory dinner. My hopes of a good meal in an air-conditioned restaurant ended up being Chinese carryout from the mall's food court. The thrill of Darken doing so well made eating food out of a cardboard box, balanced on my knee at home in front of the TV, still feel like I was celebrating. When I wondered how long it took for the queen to finally get her horse in the trailer, I couldn't help but smile. Not only did my little black fox beat her horse in the show ring, we beat it in the parking lot, too. Another day it could easily be the other way round, but today, we were victorious and we were going to savor the moment. That's what life is all about, savoring the moments when they come our way.

Chapter 21

PUTTING ON THE RITZ

NEXT WE were invited to perform for a weekend youth riding camp. I could expect forty kids who were taking part in an advanced riding improvement camp, and the location was one of the most beautiful horse farms in the nation. These kids were already very horse savvy and were attending the camp to fine tune their riding skills with expert instructors.

Darken and I were to provide Friday night's surprise entertainment. While it's always fun to use my trick horses to teach inner city kids, especially those who have never touched a horse before, this type of event was even more fun to do. It gives me a chance to show kids that horses can do much more than they are used to seeing.

This demo was going to be something special. This was not only an Arabian farm, but one of magnificent proportions and prestige. If Darken behaved like a baboon there, I would be mortified. In cases like this, my old standby, Black Tie, would usually get the gig. Not many people knew about Darken yet. I'd been keeping him on the back burner, so to speak, bringing him along slowly. However, Darken was beginning to surpass his mentor. Tie was getting older and some tricks like rearing and lying down were beginning to get harder for him and I no longer wanted to ask him to try. On the other hand, Darken was full of youthful bounce, sometimes too much bounce. Darken would go.

We made the trip to the farm and what we found amazed us. From the elegant farm entrance to the mahogany and wrought iron stalls, we found ourselves in horse paradise. I pulled my trailer around to the back door of the arena. Not one thing was out of place in this picture-perfect horse palace. In fact, the only thing out of place on the grounds was the shavings that Darken had knocked out of our trailer as I unloaded him. To maintain the perfection, I carefully swept up the shavings and tossed them back into the trailer.

I set up my equipment: the wooden boxes that Darken would hopefully stand on, the bean bag he'd hopefully sit on, and our other props. Never before had we been invited to such a magnificent farm. I was worried that we would not be up to their expectations. Would my Darken be a hit or a flop? The beauty of trick training is that it teaches your horse how to learn, and instills in him a willingness to perform for you. This willingness is necessary in order to give a smooth performance. If Darken chose not to perform, there'd be nothing I could do about it. In a few minutes, forty kids would be expecting an hour show.

The arena in which we were to perform was beautiful. The only prints in the freshly groomed sand were ours. As I walked Darken inside the arena to show him around a little before the kids got there, he bowed up his neck and snorted at each step we took. Clearly he had not recognized the importance of being invited to such a place. It took a few minutes, but he quickly settled in and was ready to go. Once his harness was on, it was show time. Once again, he surprised me by performing very well. He hopped up onto his pedestal box, sat on his bean bag, crossed his legs, bowed, lay down, and obediently pranced and danced through the rest of his tricks right on cue. I was so happy and proud of him.

Darken and I were there just for their entertainment, but I also snuck in bits of information about how trick training requires lots of patience and time, how it is a unique way to develop a close bond with your horse, and how it improves the lines of communication between horse and handler. I hoped that we instilled the importance of always being kind to their horses and rewarding them for a job well done.

When I was invited to stay for refreshments after the show, the manager of the farm offered to let me turn Darken out into one of their beautiful, white board fenced paddocks. A generous offer to be sure, but I told him that if I did, Darken wouldn't want to go back home with me. Darken went back into our trailer and spent the time enjoying his hay bag, never knowing what he missed.

The next day, I received the following messages: *You were certainly a hit last night! Kids and adults both are still talking about you today.... Heard people raving all day. One of the instructors was reminding all of the kids to remember what you said about rewarding and praising your horse at the end of their lesson session.*

These are a few of the many reasons I share my trick horses with kids. While they are being entertained, I hope they retain a little of the information that I share with them, so it will improve the time spent with their own horses.

Chapter 22

AND AWAY WE GO

WE WENT from a farm that was literally right out of a magazine to a scene right out of the Old West. We were invited to perform at a cowboy mounted action shoot. The day's shooting contest was expected to be over by 5:00 PM, and we were to provide the evening's entertainment at 6:00 PM, followed by a steak dinner. I could have arrived after the shooting stopped, but I couldn't resist going early to see how Darken would react to the gunfire. I knew that, at first, he'd come out of his skin, but I hoped that someday he might be able to participate in the sport. One look at the period cowboy clothing the riders were all wearing and I was itching to strap on a set of guns and give it a try.

We arrived early and I parked far enough away from the shooting that the gunfire sounded like dull, rapid-fire pops. Coming out of the trailer, Darken immediately heard the shots and his head jerked up. Oh dear. I took him for a meandering walk toward the ring where the shoot was going on. Rider after rider exploded at a dead run through the gate, gun drawn, as they rode a pattern, and shot at a dozen balloons. For each balloon, there were three things for Darken to deal with; a gunshot, a cloud of smoke, and the popping sound of the balloon.

The closer we got to the ring, the louder the sounds were and the more action Darken could see. Not wanting to bother any of the competition horses, I led him toward the empty south end of the grounds. At each step Darken became more and more unglued, and all eyes were beginning to turn toward us. Hoping he might think there was safety in numbers, I took him to the north end of the ring where all the other horses were. Finally, we had worked ourselves close enough that we stood right next to the rail between several other horses. I watched a few riders run the course and took a look at Darken to see how he was holding up to all of the excitement. I expected him to become more agitated by the noise, meaning I'd soon have to move him further away from the competition. I needn't have worried. He was asleep—this from a horse who once was completely unnerved when the barn cat silently popped out from under the wheelbarrow he was sniffing.

When it was time for him to entertain the cowboys and cowgirls, he once again performed like a champ. I was very proud of him. I was repaid by being invited to stay for their club's steak dinner and Darken retired to eat his own dinner of carrots and hay in his stall. It was a good way for both of us to end a fun day.

As the summer wore on, Darken, the formerly scaredy-cat colt, continued to receive invitations to perform at Pony Club camps, horse shows, community events, schools, special needs homes, fund raisers, benefits, and countless charities. Each time, he gained a little more experience and a little more confidence. We had a wonderful time going to new places and meeting new people. Whether performing for a small group of 4-H members or in front of hundreds in a packed coliseum, we always tried to put on a good show for them. Darken and his story were inspiring people and bringing them joy.

Our favorites to entertain were always children's groups. Whenever possible, after each performance I would lead Darken slowly around the rail so they could see a real live trick horse up close. To share him with others, gives me great joy. I always stop and let kids pet him and ask questions; in their eyes, I see myself fifty years ago. So many little hands reached out to touch him that each walk quickly turned into a petting session. Whenever a little hand poked out at him through the fence, Darken would stop, hang his head low, and wait so they could pet his face. He'd stop just long enough, and then move on to the next outstretched hand.

At one event, Darken performed for a large group of young "cowboy and cowgirl" campers, most about six years old. After the performance, by the time I had unharnessed Darken and put him inside our horse trailer, each child had already written me a "thank you" card. The kids had help in their writing and spelling from the camp counselors, but the drawings of a prancing Darken wearing his white harness and red plume and me smiling beside him, were all theirs. Some had drawn crude stick figures, and one child had colored Darken green, but they drew and colored from their hearts. Their efforts were greatly appreciated and I still have their cards, unable to throw them away. As part of their day's cowboy activities, the kids were trying to use strings of baler twine as lariats. The limp twine was useless, but the kids still tried to twirl them. The following day, as a "thank you" gift to them, I sent them two real cowboy lariats so they would have better success practicing their roping skills.

One gloriously sunny day, Darken and I were invited to take part in the opening ceremonies for a very prestigious annual jumper show. It was more than just a horse show; it was a gala event, complete with floral arrangements, reserved box seating, and catered refreshments for those paying to see the show. It was quite exciting to be made part of such an event. As soon as we arrived, we saw just how impressive the horses and exhibitors were. I felt like a little fish in a big pond—a very poor little fish in a very rich big pond. However, while the horses there had talents we didn't have, we had talents they didn't have. Darken wasn't a jumper, and they weren't trick horses. We would not be intimidated. Well, maybe just a little.

Waiting our turn in the shade of a big maple tree, I stood admiring Darken. He was a bit worried about his surroundings, but I was sure he'd do his best. At least I hoped so. He was wearing his white harness and had glittery red and silver streamers in his mane and tail. He sparkled in the sun. When the time came, Darken did his part of the opening ceremonies by performing a number of tricks in front of the audience. They smiled and clapped and drank their ice tea. None of them had any idea how much Darken had overcome to be able to perform for them. It made me happy to know that while he was very unsure of the situation, he performed his tricks just because I asked him. I gave a final wave as Darken gave one last bow and we left the ring, our part of the festivities done.

A few weeks later, at an event to raise money for a handicapped riding program, a lady approached me and asked if Darken could pose for a photo with her duck. It seemed like a pretty odd request, but there she stood with a brown Mallard duck in her hands. I had seen "Gramma Duck" before. A charming "Gramma and Grandpa Duck", as they called themselves, took their pet ducks to events for people to see and touch. Raised in roasting pans, of all things, three or four ducks would calmly sit in their pans set atop a baby buggy. The tame ducks were then pushed around and would stop to interact with anyone who wanted to see them. The ducks were a big hit wherever they went; who wouldn't want the opportunity to pet a gentle duck. The bravest kids were allowed to hold a duck in their outstretched hands, and the ducks were happy to sit there. Darken was more than happy to share a photo session with such goodwill ambassadors to children's education and enjoyment.

While I have trained dozens of trick horses, none of them gave me a fraction of the trouble, or required more training time, than Darken. He took a lot more effort, but it was well worth it, knowing that I had helped him discover, not only one talent, but several.

I cherish each performance with him. Each time I buckle on his harness, I can still picture him lying in my lap shortly after his birth, our stall and bucket disaster, and all the countless times I questioned my sanity in wanting to keep him. I am always glad I did.

Chapter 23

THE QUIET HORSE

ONE DAY, I noticed Darken standing alone in the pasture run-in shed. It's not unusual for all the horses to come in from the pasture to rest in its shade in the afternoon, but they all come together. The younger horses all lay down for a nap, while the older ones stand over them, taking short cat naps themselves. But on this day, Darken was standing all alone. This was unusual. All the other horses were up on the hill grazing while he stood sadly alone. Darken would never knowingly be left behind.

As a foal, he'd sometimes awake from his nap to find his mother had moved off a short distance. His head would pop up out of the tall grass, he'd search around for her, give a little whinny, and then he'd be up and off like a rocket after her. No one left Darken behind for very long.

I later caught him standing alone in the shade of a tree, then again off in the corner of the pasture. He had me worried. His mother, Spotty, acted the same way when I first noticed something was wrong. She had stood quietly off by herself, not concerned about where the rest of the herd was, content to rest and sun herself. No signs of being sick, just resting in the sun. Now Darken was doing the same thing. When the others came to eat hay, he was standing alone in the run-in shed again. When I mentioned it to my husband, he said he noticed him alone in the shed the day before too. This was getting to be a bigger concern. Darken was now five, just one year younger than his mother was when she became sick and died.

Not wanting to miss any early signs of a possible illness, I called the vet's office. The office receptionist on the phone cheerfully asked, "What is the appointment for please?" Trying to sound very professional, I said, "I'd like the vet to come and check my horse."

She sounded a bit more concerned, "Is he sick?"

I said, "No."

She asked, sounding even more worried, "Does he have colic?"

Again, I said, "No."

Now she was really puzzled, "Does he have a temperature?"

Feeling more and more like an idiot and not really wanting to say it, I said. "No. He's just acting too quiet."

For five years, I had put up with a horse that literally came unglued at the drop of a hat. And now that he was standing around being normal and quiet, I called the vet because I thought something must be wrong with him!

Silly as it sounded, I said, "Please come check my horse because he's acting normal." I had that nagging worry that he was starting to display the same signs that his mother had in the weeks before her death. I didn't care how silly it sounded, or for that matter, what it cost. I wanted the vet to come check my horse because he was acting like a normal horse, and that wasn't normal for him.

My usual vet was out of town, so the clinic sent a new vet out. I'd never met him before but he seemed very nice, as well as the student assistant he brought with him. I brought Darken out of his stall and the two men eyed him closely. Darken stood quietly, which should have been a clue right there. I imagine that they'd already had quite an interesting conversation, at my expense, on the way to my farm. They probably thought I was a nut job, but once I had explained why I'd called, they understood my concern. I was right to want to catch any problems early; I had done everything right with his mother and it sure hadn't helped her.

It took forever as the vet listened to his heart and lungs with his stethoscope. Of course, in those long agonizing minutes no one spoke. He listened here, he listened there, and he'd pause, go back and listen again someplace, which only made me think he had heard something so bad that he had to recheck it to be sure. Through it all, Darken stood quietly. In the end, everything sounded good. They took a blood sample and would call with the results.

The following day, the results were in and they were good. So good in fact, the vet said he'd be hard pressed to find anything wrong with him. Hurray, but why wasn't he acting like himself? Perhaps, he was just growing up. It had cost me $194.00 to have the vet tell me that my horse, who had finally decided it was okay to rest alone in the run-in shed, was just fine.

Chapter 24

SECOND DRESSAGE SHOW

WE HAD such great success with the first dressage show that I could hardly wait for the next one. This time we were coming into it with more knowledge and experience and feeling much more confident. I had first entered Darken in a dressage show simply because I thought it the safest way to get him into a show ring under saddle, and he turned out to have a real talent for it. Now we were getting serious.

I secretly wanted to take another whack at the dressage queen and see if my backyard pony could beat her fancy horse again. It was a private challenge to have fun with. She didn't know us from Adam, and I doubt she even noticed that we were there, but I couldn't wait; I hoped that she and her horse would be there again.

The morning of the show I went out to the barn early to give Darken a bath and found him glued to the corner of his stall. He was facing the big barn door listening to something. It wasn't all that unusual. He often stood, looking up into the rafters or at a wall, as if he heard or saw something that no one else did. His ears were pricked up and he was clearly agitated. He went from standing and listening to spinning around and around in his stall. I got him out of his stall and he was shivering all over. In the August heat he couldn't possibly be cold; it must have been from his nervousness. I'd never seen him shiver like that or spin around in his stall before. Not good and definitely not good on a horse show day.

I tied two twenty-five foot longe lines together so I could work him in a larger circle, and took him out to run a few laps in the hay field. He ran and ran and ran with no signs of slowing down or getting tired. In his agitated state, there was no way I was going to safely take him anywhere, let alone show him. Normally, once he had run around enough on the line or in the pasture to get some of the freshness out of his system, he was good to go. Not this day; there was no reasoning with him. He was excited, nervous, and kept running on his own until he was hot and sweaty. He only stopped because I stopped him, worried that he would hurt himself. He was always full of himself and high-energy, but I had never seen him act like this before. Had strangers been messing around the barn at night, or were coyotes or some other type of wild critter lurking around? I had no idea what was wrong with him and nothing I did helped solve his problem one little bit. If I knew what had scared him so badly, it might help me deal with it in the future.

Late one night last winter, I was surprised by something that flashed by in front of me as I approached the barn. I wasn't thinking about anything particular when I saw it. It appeared to be the apparition of a horse, moving quickly from left to right between myself and the barn door. I could see the tops of its legs but nothing below its knees, as it seemed to float about two feet off the ground. I just missed seeing its head, but I did clearly see its neck, back, flat croup, white mane and high flying white tail. The edges of its body were white, but the middle of its body was transparent and I could see the gray barn door behind it. It was clearly an Arabian horse by its body shape.

Had I just caught a glimpse of the ghost of Darken and Dancin's late mother who had come to visit them? Their stalls were just a few feet from where the apparition ran. Several well-loved horses lie buried on our farm in places of honor. It could have been any one of them, but I am betting it was their mother, Spotty.

I had no idea what had set Darken off this day, but he had to get over it, quickly. No time to worry about it now; I had pre-paid his entry fees, so off to the show we went. I would deal more with him there. The confidence I'd had in him was gone as I lead a jittery, ticking time bomb to the trailer. Darn it. I was hoping we were past all of this nonsense.

Thankfully, once at the show he was much better. As I was checking in, I spotted a friend who had brought her young mare to its first show. She had already shown it in one class, and I asked how she had done. She turned around to show me a black muddy spot on the back of her shoulder and hip where her mare had unceremoniously dumped her on her way to the show ring. Someone had popped out of the judge's stand, the little playhouse, and spooked her horse. Exactly the situation I was worried would happen to me!

Somehow it's always comforting when someone else gets bucked off their horse first. It means that you won't be the only one inducted into that special little club at the show. If you are the second or third rider to come off your horse, it's old news. Something about comfort in numbers, so to speak.

I checked the list of competitors and, unfortunately, my dressage queen was not entered. Showing is so much more fun if you set little goals for yourself. Beating the dressage queen again was our little goal, and now she wasn't even entered. Rats! No worries, we'd just choose another target.

Despite the bad behavior mystery that morning, overall Darken was improving by leaps and bounds. Just as his trick training had helped improve our lines of communication from the ground, his dressage training was helping him improve under saddle. Both disciplines asked him to respond to cues and, when he did, he was rewarded. Darken still had a ways to go, but more and more, I was catching glimpses of the performance horse he was becoming. He had times of brilliance, which gave me great encouragement, and times when he backslid in his training, which took the wind out of my sails. Though thrilled that his good days were far outnumbering his bad, his latest antics had me worried.

Darken placed 1st and 2nd in his two classes. He ended the day well, but I still had no idea what had been wrong with him that morning. Perhaps he'd seen another ghost!

Chapter 25

THIRD DRESSAGE SHOW

SINCE THERE was one last dressage show of the season and Darken seemed to enjoy them, we made plans to finish the series and see how we did. I sent in my entries on a bright and sunny day. It was now October in Ohio; the weather could turn at a moment's notice, and it did.

Again, I took Darken to the show grounds the day before the show for practice, and we were the only ones there. It was quite marvelous. If he acted silly, no one would be the wiser; no dressage queens to look down on us; no instructors watching us, knowing full well I had only taken a few dressage lessons. Compared to the first practice there, Darken was very calm and easygoing. I rode him around the outside of all three show rings and in the three warm-up rings. He was just fine. There was no wind to make the willow tree grab at him, the little play houses were closed up, and the bushes were no longer threats to be avoided as if his life depended on it. I even rode him inside the indoor arena, where one wall was covered in mirrors. He stood for a moment and seemed to admire the horse that looked back at him from the mirror. It sure was a handsome horse.

We were back outside in the practice ring when the owner of the show grounds drove in and parked just around the corner from us. Darken barely noticed. We were doing a lovely circle in the corner of one of the warm-up rings when Darken and I simultaneously noticed something out of the corner of our eyes. Darken made a big leap sideways and nearly went down on both knees. If he hadn't been quick as a cat about it, he would have fallen down on his left shoulder, and I would have come off over his neck. Turns out, the owner had unloaded a large bag of ice from the back of her car. As she gave it a big pull, it came flying out of the trunk and landed with a funny-sounding crunchy thud on the ground. The unexpected sound scared the stuffing out of Darken and his reaction raised my own blood pressure a few notches. I stuck with him and we continued on with our practice as if it had never happened.

By show day, it was cold and rainy and not a fun day to show at all. Still, we slogged on. While I had Darken in the barn aisle tacking him up, a young girl stood beside him watching me braid his mane. Pretty soon she was up by his head and petting him. Darken stood there taking it all in. I'd almost forgotten that he could come unglued at a moment's notice, and I normally would have had to warn kids to stay away from him. It wasn't that I was afraid that he'd intentionally harm anyone. He was a lover, not a fighter, but I was always worried that, if he backed up and bumped into someone's buckets or tack box sitting in the aisle, he might scare himself and accidentally step on someone's toes. But, since he remained calm, I let her play with him. How nice to have a normal horse. Darken warmed up well and we waited our turn to enter the ring.

The queen, with the horse who would not load, was once again not entered. I so wanted to try to beat her again, but it was not to be. However, a much better horse was there that day. He was a big bay gelding and very lovely. When I went to the entry booth to see how many horses were posted to ride in my classes, I found his name listed among them. As I was pondering that bit of unexpected news, I spotted his sales ad posted on the bulletin board. His scores were always among the highest of the day, and it was reflected by his $25,000.00 price tag. Given his qualifications and long list of accomplishments, it seemed pointless to try, but he was the one to beat.

With all the rain, the outdoor rings had large puddles and muddy spots here and there. All of the horses entered ahead of me galloped through them as if they weren't even there. I tried to remember if Darken had even stepped foot in a puddle outside of the pasture before. I didn't think so.

When it was our turn, we entered the ring and tried our best. Darken charged right in and went through those lakes of water as if he'd done it all his life. He never faltered or needed encouragement. Yet, the sight and sound of a bag of ice being unloaded from a car had nearly knocked him off his feet the day before. Our skid marks were still visible in the mud in the warm up ring. What a puzzlement. He won the class and had beaten the expected winner. I wish I could have been a fly on the wall back at their stalls when they discovered we'd beaten them. His win over such a horse gave me another huge boost of confidence in Darken's potential.

An hour later we showed in our second class. Darken put in a good effort, but this time we placed second, just behind the horse we had beaten earlier. The scores were close; we gave him a good run for his money and we were happy.

Back in his stall, all snug and wrapped up in his winter blanket, Darken stood, barely able to keep his eyes open. What a change from the horse he was at his first couple of shows. I was even able to leave the top half of his door open for the first time while I went to eat lunch.

My fellow exhibitors were cold, wet, and muddy, yet there was still a thrill in the air about being there. People in the barns were wrapped in horse blankets and clung to cups of hot coffee to try to stay warm. Yet everyone was friendly, happy, and truly interested in how each others' horses did. Despite the weather, it was one of those special days when the planets were aligned and life was just a little extra good. I was in no hurry to go home.

My husband, Charles, stayed home, warm and close to the TV and refrigerator. He understands my passion, but it's not *his* passion. One of his passions is horse power, but of the motorcycle kind. He has buddies that he rides with, so he understands what it's like when a group of like-minded people get together to share the same interests. He lets me do horses and I let him do motorcycles. It works for us.

When Darken was born, my husband was content to walk to the barn to look at him, pat him on the head, snap a few photos for me, and then retire back to the warmth of the house. I, on the other hand, stayed for hours to handle and inspect every inch of the new foal. I dabbed at his squishy pink muzzle, ran the hairs of his mane through my fingers, and laughed as I picked up his little bushy squirrel tail. I didn't need time to bond with him. I had bonded with him the moment I first saw him as a black dot on the vet's ultrasound machine. I had waited eleven months for him to be born, which gave me a lot of time to make great plans for him. I was not about to rush back to the house, now that he was actually alive and lying in my lap, just because the hour was late or the air cold.

As the dressage show wound down, I packed up my once clean tack and clothes and loaded Darken into the trailer. It would feel good to be back home, sitting on the couch with my hubby, warm, dry, and, most likely, with a bowl of hot soup. When I complained about the day's weather, hubby said, "You didn't have to go." It was that simple to him. If it's inconvenient, just don't do it, and I suppose it is just that easy. Of course, he thinks nothing of zooming down the road on his motorcycle in a cold rain just to get a cup of coffee with his friends across the state line. But go to the show I did that day, and I wouldn't have missed it for the world.

One month later, the year-end show series results were posted. In our open division, Darken finished as reserve champion, with a score of 69.131%. Our rival, the $25,000.00 horse, finished grand champion with a score of 69.783%. The series also offered a high point award for Arabians, which Darken won, 10 points above his nearest competitor.

The following year, Darken moved up from reserve to grand champion in the open division, and again won the high point Arabian award. He also would compete at his first USDF (United States Dressage Federation) rated show, winning the high score Arabian award and qualifying for, and later showing at, the Arabian and Half Arabian Sport Horse Nationals that same year.

Chapter 26

THE TRAIL RIDE

BEING NORTHEAST Ohio, the weather turned once again; perfect crisp fall weather and the trees were showing off their colors. It was a good time to hit the trails, so off we went to the site of a recent big trail ride. The annual ride-a-thon held there had been a major fundraiser for a local therapeutic riding center. I have ridden this ride for many years, often setting a goal to have a new young horse ready for its first big outing there. This provided me with a deadline so I could gauge the progress of their training to allow safe participation in such an event.

In my own mind, it was always a big day when I picked which of my young horses would go on the ride that year. It was their special "rite of passage". Could a young horse be ready to go on the ride by the first weekend in October? I liked to think they considered it a great honor to be picked and be seen by three hundred other trail riders. It was Darken's year to go, but my last dressage show had fallen on the same date. I missed the trail ride and Darken had missed his big début there.

So as not to disappoint him and miss another pretty day to trail ride, we packed up, drove an hour to the site of the missed event, and prepared for a day of enjoyment on the trails. Darken and I started out across the nearly empty parking lot quite nicely. It was going to be a good day. As we rounded the corner to head into the woods, the trail ran parallel with a busy road, on a tight curve for a hundred feet. Darken was tensely watching the cars on the road, whizzing past just feet from my right stirrup, and there was a weird sound in the air that had him further on edge. The high pitched whirring sound came from someone who was running a weed eater around their mail box post near the road. A few feet beyond that on the trail, stood a grandmother pushing a black baby buggy. The baby buggy put a stop to Darken the moment he saw it. Holy smokes! We had speeding cars, a weed eater, and now a big black baby buggy to deal with all at once. It was just too much. Darken slammed on the brakes and toyed with the idea of spinning around and returning to the safety of his trailer. The pusher of the baby buggy looked at us like we had three heads, completely unaware that she had just struck terror into the heart of a 900 pound horse.

I let Darken stand and stare, then asked him to step forward a few steps. He took one step and stopped. He stood staring a little longer then he gingerly stepped forward and skirted out and around the dreadful buggy. Thankfully, the lady stood still and let us around her. Once past the buggy of doom, we were happily on our way down the trail, but both our hearts were still pounding. Darken, because of all the unexpected frights, and I, because of what he might do in response to them. We had a rush of adrenalin that lasted for a few minutes, but quickly put our troubles behind us.

It was wonderful to be out enjoying the day and soon our hearts were singing. The trails were wide and clear, the sky was blue, and butterflies were everywhere, including one that landed on the end of Darken's nose. I saw it fluttering toward us and I watched with horror as it flew straight into the middle of his muzzle. Darken gave a startled flip of his head and sent the big yellow critter flying to land somewhere safer.

I found a pretty little waterfall and thought that it was a good spot to take a photo. I maneuvered Darken out into the middle of the creek; another one of my plans that seemed a good idea at the time. Since the algae covered rocks were slippery, I dismounted and led him out across them and snapped a few photos of him standing in the creek. When I turned around to leave, I suddenly found myself on my hands and knees in the water. My feet had gone out from under me so fast I had no time to try to catch myself. My camera went into the water and hit the rocks below so hard the batteries fell out. I snatched everything up and we got out of there quick. Once on dry land, I quickly looked around to make sure that no one had seen me fall. Thankfully, they hadn't. I dried off the camera, put the batteries back in, and remounted; we were good to go again.

Once again it was a dumb move on my part. Darken could have easily fallen and gotten hurt and then what would I have done? As it was, we were lucky to get out of the river with just my boots and pant legs getting wet and the camera taking a bath. As it turned out, in the end, he and I and the camera lived to tell the tale.

Back on the trail and off the slippery rocks, we had a wonderful time enjoying the trails. I enjoyed the fact that Darken had progressed to the point where I no longer feared a panicked bucking spree. In truth, not counting our stall and bucket disaster, he had only bucked with me once. I never had even come close to falling off him, yet, it was something I still thought about. He might become startled, spook at something unexpected, or overreact to something he considered alarming (even if it was just a candy wrapper blowing across the trail); I noticed that I was becoming more relaxed and trusting of him. It was a nice feeling.

As we walked along, not in any hurry to go home, we ran into little groups of other riders now and then. Everyone always said, "Hello, what a pretty horse," to each other as we passed. We would have said it even if the other horse was homelier than a picket fence. They didn't have to tell me that my horse was pretty; I already knew it, just as the riders of all the other horses also knew they had the best horse on the trails that day.

Throughout the day we came across a wide variety of horses and riders. Men riders dressed in cowboy attire who tipped their hats to us as they passed, middle aged ladies in comfortable clothes who always had a smile and good word for us, and teenagers who usually are more absorbed in conversation among themselves to take much notice of us, as we practically rubbed stirrups with them on a narrow trail.

We came across a grandmother riding a white draft cross, out enjoying the day with her young granddaughter on a tiny gray pony. Both ladies were dressed in smart, formal English attire and were repeating a scene that could have been from 2010, 1910, or even 1810—one older horsewoman passing down her knowledge to an obviously horse-crazy little girl. It made me wonder if that love of horses had skipped a generation in their family, leaving mom and dad at home with more interest in boating, golfing, or watching TV than in mastering the fine art of horsemanship. They had no idea what they were missing. Interesting the things one thinks about as one rides along.

On our way back to the parking lot, we rounded a corner and came face to face with two other black horses with four high white stockings and snips on their noses. The other riders also noticed that their horses were marked nearly identically to Darken. Black horses with four high white stockings are not that common in the horse world. Here we were, three of us, suddenly standing face to face on the trail. I had to snap a photo. My horse was a little shorter than theirs, so they said if their two horses had a baby, it would look like mine.

When I was a child, I would paint white legs on my black plastic model horses, making them my favorites. Little did I know at the time, fifty years later, I would be riding a real stocking-legged black horse.

You just never know what is around that next corner in life. It could be a scary black baby carriage, an unexpected dunk in the river, seeing a field of butterflies, or a chance meeting of your identical twin. That's what makes life interesting and keeps you looking around that next corner with a little bit of fear, but always hoping for the best.

Chapter 27

THE FUN SHOW

I LEARNED of a "fuzzy fun" horse show to be held a few hours away. It was a schooling show, billed as a good place for beginner riders, or those starting young horses to get them into the show ring for a day of fun. That sounded right up Darken's alley and just what he needed next in his journey.

Since he had surprised me with his good behavior and talent at the dressage shows, I was anxious to see what else he might be good at. My problem horse had already shown me he could do much more than I ever expected he would be capable of. Now that he was proving that he could compete with the best of them, I wanted him to be able to spread his wings a little more. At worst, it would be a learning experience for him. At best, it would show me a few more of his talents yet undiscovered. I got out my map and made plans to attend the show.

I had never been to the show grounds before and drove past the hidden driveway twice before I finally found it. The narrow driveway went up a hill and curved behind an auto body shop. The chain link fence lining the driveway was rusted and overgrown with dead vines and weeds, giving me a bad feeling about this remote and hidden little show grounds. However, once I rounded the top of the hill a lovely white board show ring lay before me. How wonderful; a real pearl in a clam shell.

Darken came out of the trailer snorting with excitement at being in a new place. He pranced around on the end of his lead, as I took him on his pre-show walk around the grounds so he could see everything. There were lots of young horses at the show, all nervous and unable to stand still. The show would be great experience for all of them.

Darken wasn't too sure about the place and what all the other horses were doing. Once under saddle and in the practice ring, he was ready to take flight. Horses were zooming all around him. I could feel the eyes of spectators on us. Either they were planning to stay out of our way or getting a good seat to see what would happen next. I wasn't real sure what was going to happen next, either. We just kept walking around the ring and slowly Darken began to relax.

He was an old hand at showing in halter, so I took him in that class first to help settle him in. He placed second in a class of sixteen all breed horses. The class included a number of other young horses, most of which were screaming their heads off since they now found themselves separated from their stable mates left back at their trailers.

Next was his English pleasure class. Darken had been ridden in a show ring before, but only in dressage, a class in which each horse shows by himself. This would be his first time showing under saddle in a ring full of other horses. Most of them were there for the additional experience and practice, just like we were. Darken was doing pretty well until he spotted a big, black, lady's handbag someone had left sitting all alone on the bleachers. He eyed that thing as if he expected it to leap over the rail at him at any moment. It took some fast talking on my part to convince him the purse was safe enough that he could walk past it. The noise of the other horses' hooves pounding the ground as they cantered up behind us scared him a bit, but Darken turned in a pretty respectable performance. He placed second in a class of fifteen. One of the more experienced Arabians beat us, but we beat the rest of them.

Between classes, Darken stood tied to the trailer. Well, stood isn't exactly the right word for it. He spent the better part of his day digging a hole to China. He's normally not a pawer at home, but when anxious, horses sometimes feel safer keeping on the move. Being tied to the trailer, Darken was prevented from walking, so he kept his legs moving the only way he could. He pawed and pawed and pawed. He'd paw with his right leg for awhile, and then switch to his left leg. Several times he got mixed up as to which leg he should be using and just held it straight out in the air in front of himself. He pawed so much that he flung dirt all over my saddle and everything else I had set out behind him to use. He'd stop for a moment, grab a bite of hay from his hay bag, and get back to work digging. Several times I caught him with his feet on top of my trailer fender, and I noticed a few teeth marks along the edge of the trailer door. I guess that he'd gotten bored with digging and eating. If I sat beside him reading a book, he was happy. He was happier yet if I would take him out to eat grass. He was very happy to do that. I wasn't sure who was training who.

[141]

Thank goodness I had parked in the back line of trailers so he was pretty hidden from prying eyes. Suddenly, there was a big commotion, a lot of banging, and people yelling, "Whoa. Whoa. Whoa." A horse, tied to a neighboring trailer, had gotten his rope tangled up and had pulled one of the back doors right off his trailer. It never fails; if there is a way to cause some excitement, horses will find it.

After watching a very competitive group of horses and riders in the class before me, I entered Darken in his first western pleasure class. I would be competing against this same group of riders. We were here; we'd give it a try. He rode like a champ in the class and did much better than I expected. He placed first out of a class of ten very nice horses, despite taking a few steps on a wrong lead, which the judge apparently missed seeing.

A few weeks later it was time for Darken's first real performance show under saddle. He had been to this show grounds before, but only for the halter classes. As I walked him around the grounds, the storm drains, which had caused him so much concern in the past, only deserved a passing glance. He knew they were there, had studied them carefully, and had decided that they weren't so bad. If a troll was to suddenly pop out of them, he'd be ready, but he kept his composure.

Being early, I was able to practice with Darken in the ring before the show started. After a good look at everything, he warmed up easily. The sight and sound of running horses no longer bothered him and he joined the traffic of the crowded ring without a worry.

Back at his stall, I readied him for his first class. This would be his first performance shown saddleseat. This class would be judged on his movement, obedience, and manners as he walked, trotted, and cantered both directions of the ring. How fun it was to tack him up in his "big horse" shiny, patent leather show bridle with double reins. I put on my red day coat and stepped up onto his back. It was the first time I had worn such a long show coat on him. It hung nearly to my knees. Last year, such a flapping coat would have frightened him, but he didn't bat an eye. I was concerned that he just might not have noticed it yet; I tested him by riding him up and down the barn aisle, trying to make it flap in the breeze. He didn't seem to mind as it billowed out around him. A few laps in the warm-up pen to test the waters even further, and we were ready for his class.

Darken boldly trotted into the ring with confidence and performed like the show horse I had always hoped he would someday be. He ignored the bleachers, the announcer's stand, the flag pole, and the trash cans along the rail. Just last year, these ordinary things were cause for concern and to be avoided at all costs. To the bystanders, the horses all looked the same as they obediently worked in the ring, but I knew differently. It had taken us a long time to reach yet another one of our goals, but, oh, what a feeling when we were finally there.

That day, the feeling of satisfaction far outweighed any award he might have won. In fact, I was so proud of his latest accomplishment that I forgot what place ribbon he had won. He didn't win the class, but what I had won was far more important to me. I had won a horse that had become a joy to own and ride. We had faced some mighty big obstacles in his first five years and we had conquered them, together. Darken had finally grown up.

Chapter 28

BACK TO THE TRAILS

SHOW SEASON was over, Darken's trick demos and clinics were done, and it was time to just let our hair down and have some fun trail riding. Another summer had passed and we were again enjoying the last of the fall trail riding season. We enjoy this time of year because the trails are free of biting green-headed horse flies and the horrid little brown deer flies that give horses no peace. It had been a full year since Darken made his first solo trail ride in the gulf. It seemed only fitting to enjoy the last days of his second fall riding season there again, getting in a few last rides before the snow flew and the river rose.

A year can really make a difference in a young horse's life, and I was happily reaping the benefits of Darken's training. Once again, the ladies invited us to join them on a trail ride. This time, Darken was better prepared with more riding time and experience under his belt. He unloaded from the trailer and barely noticed the other horses in the parking lot. He even failed to notice that a dark chestnut gelding named Blaze would be joining us for the first time. We all saddled up and headed out to the trails.

First stop was the dreaded cement blocks. This time, it was Blaze who refused to walk between them. Darken easily walked through and looked back over his shoulder as if to say, "What's the fuss?" It took a little convincing, but Blaze finally skittered through and we were on our way. All was well until we reached the first narrow ravine. This was the first time Darken had seen water flowing through the bottom of the ravine, and slippery leaves lined its muddy banks. To be safe, I dismounted and led Darken across. He leaped across it easily. Blaze would have none of it and refused to cross. It took a lot more convincing and encouragement with a short crop before he finally leaped across.

The next trouble spot was the steep ravine. This was the same one that Darken and I had attempted last year when he'd caught a stick under the cheek piece of his bridle, my rope had caught in his tail, and my pant leg had snagged on the loose cantle plate on the back of his saddle, as we attempted to slide down the ravine into the water. This time, Darken sat and slid down the muddy slope into the river below without hesitation. Again, Blaze had second thoughts. He got half way down the slope and wheeled around in the hope of going anywhere but down into the river. He was a seasoned trail horse, but these were new trails for him and they unnerved him. His rider had to dismount and lead him down the hill and into the water, getting her jeans wet to the knees, before remounting. How nice it felt to be sitting on my faithful little horse at the bottom of the hill watching and waiting for the rest to catch up.

This day, after a recent rain, the river level was up and moving a little faster than my liking. Had I been alone, I would not have crossed. I do make some good decisions now and then. But in the company of others who wanted to forge across ahead of us, we carefully followed along behind. The water was muddy and deep, making it impossible to see the rocks and ledges below the surface. I followed the horses ahead of me, trying to keep Darken stepping where they had just stepped, carefully trying to avoid anything unexpected. On the third of the eight river crossings, we were carefully picking our way across when, mid-river, Darken and I spotted the same rock. Unfortunately, he spotted it a split second before I did. In the dark river water, filled with dark brown rocks, he noticed the only big white boulder under the surface, just as he stepped past it. He must have thought there was something in the water about to grab his legs, as he leaped straight out of the water with all four feet in the air like a scalded cat. In truth, I could not blame Darken, as I would have done the same thing. Even to me, the white rock looked very out of place and alive under the muddy water. Already afraid that he'd trip over an unseen rock and I'd go over his head into the rushing water, I had taken the precaution of holding onto my saddle's grab strap. That trusty little loop of leather, buckled to the front of my saddle, saved me from taking a cold bath that day.

We ladies and our horses rode along, enjoying the day and each other's company. Blaze decided that our trails were pretty much like the ones he'd been on before and willingly covered hill and dale without any more fuss or silliness. We rode on to the end of the trails and then retraced our hoof prints back to our trailers. We were done, the last ride of the year; we had used our time wisely and could now reflect on all our season's trail riding adventures.

However, the days continued to be sunny; each day that the sun shone seemed an invitation to hit the trails one more time. Each time Darken and I went, I thought it would be the last before the cold rains and snow hit. The river was still safe to cross, but soon it would be too deep, too fast, and too dangerous. Each last ride was to be savored slowly, as its memories would have to last all winter.

As luck would have it, Mother Nature gave us one more picture-perfect day before the cold rains started and we'd have to resort to indoor riding. Darken and I packed up for one last fall ride, just the two of us, with the sun on our faces and its warmth embracing us. The weather report was calling for bad weather just around the corner, so off we went. The gulf was close to home and even though we had ridden there several times recently, it was so beautiful that we chose it again for our last ride.

Darken and I hit the trails with the intention of enjoying every moment and looking at every little piece of nature, and we did. The leaves were mostly gone from the trees now. They were wet and flattened, with just a touch of crunch left to them. They carpeted the ground, mixed with the smell of rotting logs and wet dirt, producing an aroma intoxicating to nature lovers. There was the odd little sprig of a green tree left here and there, but the rest of the woods were bare. No more falling acorns, only the ones the squirrels hadn't hidden away yet, lay blanketing the ground and crushed underfoot. You could look through the trees now to see things you had missed when the leaves and brush were thick. We took our time and wandered through the rarely used trails that were off the beaten track. We found the remains of a shelter someone had built out of cut branches. It was quite an elaborate structure that had been completely hidden by leaves all summer. The shelter was now in disrepair and only the door hung straight.

Last year Darken was terrified of every sight and sound in the woods, but now he stood up on a ridge and looked out across the valley like he owned the place. Last year he would not have wanted to stop and stand still; now he was content to stand quietly, his eyes and ears scanning the valley below, until I asked him to move on. Was it just last year I had one of those ears in my mouth? Yes, I believe it was. I can still taste it. These were the same ears I had once admired and held in the palm of my hand while they were still wet, shortly after his birth. As a colt, they peeked up through short, curly, black ringlets. Now, as a five year old, they stuck up through a mass of long and heavy mane. I'd spent the better part of the past two years seeing the world framed by those two black ears. Not once in his five years did he ever lay them back at me in annoyance or anger. He greeted me each morning with his ears forward, happy, and ready to take on the day. Sitting on his back, looking out between those ears at the trees beyond reminded me of another old Arab proverb—*The wind of Heaven is that which blows between a horse's ears.*

We stopped often just to sit, look, and listen. I wanted to soak in everything so the memories would last, not only through the winter months, but for the rest of my life.

Thirty-two years earlier I had experienced such a moment when my son, Shawn, was just a newborn. I was standing in line with my mother at the grocery store holding him in my arms. I looked down at him and thought, "I am going to remember this moment for the rest of my life." It seemed silly at the time. Surely it was not note-worthy enough to remember longer than a few minutes. There were going to be more important times in his life that I would remember better—his graduation, his wedding, and the birth of his children. I have many fond memories of him as a baby, but this one, so sim-ple and ordinary, stands out just because it was so ordinary. But, I remember that moment like it was yesterday. I can still see, in my mind's eye, his blond hair peeking up out of the brand new light-blue blanket my mother had given me as gift for him. He was wrapped in that same blanket when I brought him home from the hospital. How wonderful to be able to think back and still see everything so clearly. I am glad I took the time to notice and remember the small things. I still have that well-worn blanket, as well as a lock of his baby-fine blond hair, lovingly wrapped in white tissue paper in my hope chest, where I keep all the other mementos of his childhood.

My mind back on the day's trail ride, I reflected on everything Darken and I had been through in his first five years—the highs and lows, the happiness and the sadness, the wins and the losses. Through it all, we had trudged on. He and I had spent a lot of time together to get where we were that day; way more time than with any oth-er horse I trained. Like his first dressage win, we had earned it and we were going to savor it. We listened to the birds, smelled the wet leaves, and admired the waterfalls. I picked flower seeds to take home and plant along the fence line.

I made another mental note to myself, "Take a good look. You are going to remember these moments for the rest of your life." We spent a lot of time riding up to the top of the next hill and just sitting and looking. We took one last long lingering look across the valley, trying to capture the image before it was covered with a layer of snow for the winter. Many years later I wanted to be able to sit in my rock-er on the front porch and still envision how the trees looked and how the fallen leaves sounded underfoot as we rode along. I wanted to remember the feel of the reins in my hand, the smell of good leather, and the way Darken's soft warm sides felt against my legs. Winning ribbons was nice, but it is the little things we often don't take time to appreciate that are the real prizes of our lives. I would be sure to appreciate them more often.

Darken stood on the ridge, head up, eyes intently looking at something across the river, his coat warm and brilliant in the afternoon sun. We both gave a deep sigh of satisfaction. The horse, that was once afraid of his own shadow, and I now stood atop the ridge and immersed ourselves in the beauty of the trails we had just traveled and I reflected on all that it had taken to get us to this day.

It had been an interesting five years, to say the least. Given his own choice, Darken probably never would have left the comfort and security of his own little pasture. But, with my help and encouragement he ventured out of his little world and traveled all across the country, doing things I never thought possible for him, and he ended up loving it and being loved. He changed my life, as well as the lives of the many people who saw him perform and heard his story. He continues to do so, to this day.

When Darken was born I had wrongly assumed that, since both his parents were champions, he would be too, on their merits alone. I discovered that he had to make it on his own, in his own way, in his own time. By slowing down, listening, and watching him closely each day, I was able to see, really see, him learn, grow, and blossom. It was an amazing process and all it took was the right encouragement to help him find what he enjoyed doing.

He overcame accidents and illnesses, never feeling sorry for himself or looking back. From his rocky start under saddle, he had gone on to win many awards, ribbons, and even had a number of championships under his belt. He had been a constant source of contradiction and amazement which kept me in a continuous state of wonder. Although he gave me a few gray hairs, he never failed to put a smile on my face.

Whenever I catch a glimpse of him in the pasture, I stop for a moment just to watch him, and it always makes me feel good. While I will most likely never become rich or famous, we have found our niche in life, and there is great comfort and satisfaction in that. We will continue to ride the trails and go to shows and chase those silk ribbons just for the fun of it. But more importantly, through the use of his tricks, Darken and I will continue to entertain and educate children. We will do our best to keep alive the traditions of famous TV cowboy role models; respect for yourself and others.

I will share Darken's story of his challenges and roadblocks. He was so afraid of the world he could have easily missed being the star that he was later to become. Darken's sister, Dancin, will tell her story too. Things came much easier to her. Yet like everyone else, she had her own difficulties to overcome before becoming a star, both in the show ring and as a trick horse.

We still have lots of dreams and adventures to chase, most of which we are not even aware of yet. Darken and I will someday travel to the world show again, and try to capture that elusive world grand championship title. We may never win it, but we will have fun trying, and that is the important part. Long after that trophy has lost its luster, I will remember all the good times we had together. There will most likely be some sadness and heartbreak along the way, but we will deal with it, if and when it comes. For every up there is a down, but thankfully, for almost every down there is also an up. We will get through the downs together and savor each and every up.

We crossed the river once more; as we started up the steep bank on the other side, we rode through a small patch of arctic air. I could feel the blast of cold air on my arm and on the hand that held the reins. The sun was shining and the temperature everywhere else was warm. It was odd enough for me to stop and try to find out why it was so cold in just that one small spot. I looked at the grasses along the trail and there was no movement. I looked up the river to see if it was acting as a wind tunnel, yet not even the slightest breeze could be felt. We rode out of the cold spot as quickly as we had ridden into it. I could still see Darken's muddy hoof prints in the mud under the shallow water at the river's edge, and tracking up the bank where we had just come. I turned him around and retraced his hoof prints, hoping to repeat the experience. I could not. What we experienced was a brief, isolated, arctic cold spot in a space the size of my horse. Then it occurred to me that the trails were named for the paths along the river used by the Native Indians. Could it be that we had just experienced a brief encounter with one of their spirits, a time overlap of sorts? How wonderful it was to think that an ancient Indian on his pony might have just occupied the same space that we had, both of us crossing the river and coming up onto the opposite bank together. I am not sure what it was, but I would like to think it was an Indian on his favorite pinto pony, out enjoying one last fall day before the snow fell.

A hundred years from now, I hope that someone on their horse, enjoying the last of the fall days in the gulf, will ride into a small patch of icy air and wonder if they had just encountered the spirit of that famous little black pinto horse that used to ride these trails and entertain so many people. The little horse who not only could, but did.

AUTHOR BIO

Jan Sharp is a freelance writer, clinician, riding instructor, and author of the book *Trick Training Your Horse To Success*. She has trained exhibition trick horses for over 40 years and has shown them to 28 world and reserve world championships. She lives in Ashtabula, Ohio with her husband, Charles, and their 21 pinto horses.

Every horse deserves to be called a champion; if not on the race track or in the show ring, at least in his owner's heart.— Jan Sharp